Dear God, HELP!
I Need A Rescue

Betty J. Simpson

To my dear Friends Sandee and Ron
Joy and Blessings to you !
Betty J. Simpson

All Scripture quotations, unless otherwise indicated, are from The Holy Bible, New International Version®, NIV® Copyright © 1973, 1978, 1984, 2011 by Biblica, Inc.™ Used by permission. All rights reserved worldwide.

Name: Simpson, Betty J.

Title: Dear God, HELP! I Need A Rescue

ISBN: 978-1-952369-26-1

Subjects: 1. Religion; 2. Christian Life: Inspirational

Published by EA Books Publishing

a division of Living Parables of Central Florida, Inc. a 501c3

EABooksPublishing.com

Dedication

This book is dedicated to Jesus the Savior, because He rescued me. Without Jesus I would be drunk or dead today. With Him I am fully alive, immersed in His love. I believe God called me to write this book, using my story to talk about who Jesus is and why knowing Him is the answer to all questions about how to best live through life's difficult times.

All of the credit goes to Jesus, who is the Author of Life and the Supplier of Words.

Table of Contents

CHAPTER 1

Introduction

Everyone has a story to tell. If you and I were meeting each other right now in person, we might be asking questions and sharing our stories. Since we're meeting through words on paper as I tell you about myself, I want you to know that I hope to hear your story, too. Please think of me as a friend who is sharing my thoughts and feelings with you. You may identify with some of them, and you may also have wondered about the same things I have. You'll see how my questions in life were answered and how I've learned to trust God—even against the odds. I hope what I share will be an encouragement to you and make a difference in your life.

I see my life in two parts: Before I met Jesus and after. He made that much of a difference! I'm a Christian now, and I have a faith that to me is worth more than gold. I hope as you read this book, you'll see Jesus Christ in new and more meaningful ways. I pray He will inform your heart, your mind, and your life's experiences as He has done for me.

The Folder

There's a folder in my closet with a piece of paper hanging from it marked "Very Important" in big colorful letters. The folder itself is labeled "Divine Medicine," with a note that says, "If I'm in the hospital, bring this folder and read everything in it to me over and over."

The folder holds a collection of things I've learned after 30 years of belonging to Jesus and studying the Bible, along with favorite Bible verses I know will fortify my faith. There are also some things I've written about the wonders of God and why I trust Him with my life.

When my daughter-in-law Rebecca saw the folder, she asked if she could have a copy of everything in it. I said yes, but I thought I should organize all of the separate pieces of paper first. Then, I joined a Beth Moore Bible study called "Entrusted" at Scottsdale Bible Church. During that study, God gave me an assignment to put the contents of my "Divine Medicine" folder into a book.

This book is the result, and it includes the priceless truth God has entrusted to me, along with the stories of what Jesus has done in the lives of my family and others. It is as much for me as it is for my readers. My goal is to strengthen my faith and yours, as we let God's truth sink into our minds and come alive in our hearts.

"For the Lord gives wisdom,
and from his mouth come knowledge and understanding."
Proverbs 2:6

A New Direction

Jesus rescued me first from myself, and second, from alcohol. Sometimes God takes his hands off the wheel and lets people run their lives into the ground so they'll come to the end of themselves and see that they can't live without

Him. Many people need to see that the things they're filling their lives with (prestige, money, possessions, alcohol, etc.) are never going to completely satisfy them. At this point, hopefully they'll turn to the only real God—the God who created them, loves them, and has been waiting all along for their hearts to belong to Him.

Well, of course I wasn't interested in knowing that! I was living "my way," never knowing or caring that God had a plan for my life that would be incredibly better. I'll be honest: I was too busy partying, spending, envying, and falling for the "If I just had ____, then I'd be happy" lie.

As my life became more and more unmanageable, I wanted something to really matter to me and take me in a new direction. While I was looking for the unknown (and not looking for God), Jesus came along out of the clear blue and called me by name.

I've told my story at Gracespring Bible Church in Richland, Michigan, at two Bible study classes in Scottsdale, Arizona, and now I'm sharing it with you to show you how God's tender love and compassion for a depleted, floundering soul in great anguish brought profound relief and changed everything!

God sent his Son, Jesus, to die on the cross in payment for my many sins. Jesus took an imperfect, flawed person (me), who wasn't interested in being counted as a follower of His, forgave me, and welcomed me into His Father's family. He gave me a brand-new life I never dreamed possible, one bubbling over with joy.

I'm still far from perfect, but my life is secure, and my goal is to help others find the peace and the gift of new life with Jesus, who loves us, warts and all.

"'...I know you by name.'"
Exodus 33:17

"'Come follow me, Jesus said...'"
Matthew 4:19

"'Come to me, all you who are weary and burdened,
and I will give you rest.'"
Matthew 11:28

CHAPTER 2

God Rescues an Alcoholic

If you and I were continuing our initial introduction in person, I would tell you I love being a wife, a mother, and a grandmother. I looked forward to each of those roles when I was young, and I adore my family.

I've always enjoyed music and art. I loved drawing floor plans of homes I thought I'd like to live in some day. While growing up, I was a first-chair violinist in an award-winning high school orchestra, and I continued to play the violin during college.

After college, I worked in an office furniture store, selling furniture and designing office layouts. When my husband and I bought our home in Michigan, I drew the floor plans for the renovations that we did. To make sure the builder was on the same page we were, without an architect, I built a to-scale foamboard model of exactly what we wanted. I also designed a contemporary, round stained-glass window for our home.

In recent years, I designed, made, and sold one-of-a-kind 'wearable art' jewelry, using sterling silver and natural gemstone beads.

If I'm making myself sound 'put together' or 'well rounded,' it's not true at all. There was a point in the midst of the good things I'm describing when it all came crashing down. That's the part I want to tell you about now—how it fell apart and how I was rescued. Instead of 'how,' I should say 'who' rescued me, because it was Jesus, whose specialty is saving people. He picked up the broken pieces of the wreck I'd made and showed me how to live the life He had planned for me.

Suddenly I had a purpose; I had peace, and I was content. I felt an exciting new anticipation for what lay ahead with Jesus at the wheel. Because of what happened to me, I want to encourage you that no matter what your struggles are or how down and depressing your life may be, there is hope. You can trust God. I learned to do it, and you can, too.

Wit's End

When I was young, I read in a fashion magazine that a woman can never be too thin, too tan, or too rich. As crazy as it may sound, I thought those were great goals. I just wanted to be somebody special. I always worried about what other people thought of me. It never occurred to me to worry about what God thought of me.

My brother, sister, and I grew up in an idyllic small town on Lake Michigan in a big house with a front staircase and a back staircase that was so steep most of us fell down those stairs more than once. Dad was a mailman who never complained about anything, even when walking his mail route in rain, snow, and ice.

Mom was a talented stay-at-home mom, who, by herself, completely redecorated our entire house—from refinishing all of the wood floors, front staircase and railing, to painting and wallpapering every wall in the house, along with making slipcovers for the sofa and curtains for all of the windows. She made beautiful braided rugs in the style of Early American décor that she loved. She dyed old wool coats into lovely colors, cut them into strips and braided them together into a pre-planned color scheme. Antique dealers would trade pieces of furniture for mom's rugs. Dad was a musician and played his baby grand piano daily, filling our home with classical music.

As kids, I remember asking dad at night if we were "scraping the bottom of the barrel," or if we had enough money for ice cream (I don't remember of him ever saying there was no money for ice cream). Then, my brother and sister and I would run upstairs and lie across mom's and dad's bed because we could watch out the window from there and see him walk two blocks to a corner store to get a pint of ice cream which he would divide five ways and bring upstairs on a tray so we could all sit on the bed and have ice cream together. A pint—not a quart—split five ways, and we were thrilled with it.

Our family went to church every Sunday. The church was on the other side of a ravine in our back yard. Dad was the church organist. Hearing him play the magnificent pipe organ was the one and only thing I liked about church. Everything else was boring. I believed in God and thought going to church was a good idea, but my understanding of God was vague.

My parents didn't argue; I never heard either of them use a swear word, even when quoting someone who had. They didn't drink or smoke. One of the things I so clearly remember was dad coming home with a Christmas gift of alcohol from someone on his mail route and mom pouring it down the drain. That picture sticks in my mind. She said her parents didn't drink, and when she was young there were two uncles who, when they came to visit, would arrive inebriated. She'd been afraid of them.

Once when I was young, a very intoxicated man came to our front door. Those were the days when no one locked their doors—at least not during the day. When my brother and I went to see who was at the door, mom told us it was a man who was drunk, and with a bit of panic in her voice, she said to me, "Run quickly and lock the screen porch door and the back door in case he tries to get in that way!" I did, and then we watched the man stagger down the street from our front window until we couldn't see him anymore. Children don't forget things like that.

We didn't have a television. I found "American Bandstand" fascinating when I got a glimpse of it at a friend's house, and I wished I could watch it at home. But my mother's father said that television would be the death of America, so she wouldn't change her mind. Although I remember my folks playing a card game called Canasta once with friends, it seemed to me that playing cards was frowned upon, as was dancing. Most of my relatives felt that mom ran a "tight ship," but she loved us, and my memories of home and childhood are good.

I was raised knowing I would go to Western Michigan University which was an hour away from our home. I felt so overprotected during my high school years that I couldn't wait to leave and make my own decisions, although I had absolutely no previous experience. Zero.

And off to college I went. Among all her other talents, mom could sew with perfection. She made absolutely gorgeous clothes for me and I arrived at my dorm well dressed. Hidden in my suitcase was a beautiful purple ceramic ashtray shaped like a canoe with crackled glass in the bottom. I bought it at the gift shop where I worked over that summer. I tried smoking once in high school at a friend's house, but I gagged and felt dizzy. Nevertheless, I thought smoking was 'movie star cool' and planned to smoke as soon as I got to my dorm. And I did. My allowance for incidentals (in 1960) was a dollar a week and it went for cigarettes, which were 25 cents per pack.

My parents never knew I smoked; I blamed my roommates for the smell of smoke on my clothes. Many years later, at a family gathering, I mentioned that I smoked in college and my mother was visibly shocked and upset. She shook her head and said, "Oh no! I don't want to hear that!"

I smoked for five or six years until I met my husband, Charlie. He said he didn't like to kiss girls who smoked, and my attraction to him was so strong I quit immediately! Whew, what a blessing that turned out to be, and in more ways than one.

On my own in college, and afterwards when working, my church attendance was sporadic until Charlie and I were married. He was raised with the wonderful habit of never missing church unless sick in bed or dead, and I was happy to go with him even though for me it was still boring. My mind wandered all over the place when I was in church, planning meals for the week, planning what I would wear to parties, or redecorating our house, etc.

Sometimes I sat there and wondered about important things, too, like how can a person get into heaven, and, is it possible to know for sure if you're going or not? Is there really a hell? Why do bad things happen? My questions were not answered, yet I felt I did something worthwhile just by being in church. Then I went home and rarely thought about God until the next Sunday.

As the years went on, I lived with increasing anxiety. It came every day and stayed for no tangible reason. I had more material things than I'd ever had before, but soon realized the things I thought would make me happy really didn't. When I was enamored with something new, the fascination wore off way too fast, and I was left wanting something else. There was a definite void in my life, and I didn't know what it was. I was nervous about everything and obsessed with worry.

Marriage wasn't exactly what I dreamed it would be. And there were aspects of parenting that were a mystery to me. Yet, on the outside, our family probably looked like an average family. We went to church, my husband had a good job, I volunteered at school, and our two boys played sports. But, on the inside we were quite disheveled, and I was the reason.

When the boys were young, my husband and I took a fabulous trip to France and Italy, thanks to his career with a pharmaceutical company. We were wined and dined, as they say, and that was my introduction to wine. Big, big, mistake. It happened slowly in the years after the trip that wine became necessary to calm my nervous butterflies. Eventually, it also became a prison with a padlock. Combination unknown.

Wow, what a tiring way of life it is when you can't shake your fears or quench your thirst for who-knows-what and the only answer that seems to work is smoothing things over with wine and pretending all is well. I did it for quite a while, but of course it meant living a lie and trying to beat down the new worries about losing my mind.

There was a period of time when I was at my absolute worst. I cried for days on end. I had such a hard time coping with life, and the knots in my stomach, that sometimes I couldn't even come out of the bedroom during the day. I used to make Charlie promise that if I ended up in a psychiatric unit, he wouldn't let them give me shock treatments. The truth was, though, I thought being in a psych unit (in my own little world) and not having to deal with anything else might be the only way to get relief from my misery.

Then I began to worry I would commit suicide and my children would blame themselves. I pictured sitting on the floor of the shower, having slit my wrists, watching the blood run down the drain. I'm sorry my sons will read this now and know what a sad mental state their mother endured. (But maybe they knew more than I thought.)

I was shallow, stubborn, and prideful. When I poured a glass of wine, I said to myself, "I'll have this if I want to and nobody can tell me not to!" The glass or two of wine I relied on every day had turned into a bottle or more of wine a day and I became something no one ever sets out to be—an alcoholic. I never ever admitted it, though, not even to myself. The more I drank the more out of control I felt; yet the more I needed to drink. The pitiful part was, I thought my life would be over if I had to quit drinking. I drank to escape, but it was a trap.

> *"Do not gaze at wine when it is red,*
> *when it sparkles in the cup,*
> *when it goes down smoothly!*
> *In the end it bites like a snake and*
> *poisons like a viper."*
> Proverbs 23:31-32

You might wonder where my husband was in all of this. Did he know what a mess I was? He was busy doing what he thought he should be doing. He was making the most of his career and providing for his family. Whether he was traveling internationally for his job or at home, work was his focus. He drank too, but he slept like a rock and was up early and off to work, feeling fine. Somehow, he didn't see that his wife was sliding down a very slippery slope.

It's amazing that no matter what your issues may be, some people have the propensity to dig themselves in deeper and deeper until they're buried. I was pretty much at my wit's end; scared to death and desperately in need of relief, peace of mind, and some answers.

What I didn't know was that being at my wit's end was exactly where God wanted me to be, so that I would give up, call Him, and say yes to meeting His Son, Jesus, the Savior. I remember being in bed, miserable from drinking too much and thinking, "I am a disaster." And then I did call out to God. With tears in my eyes, I prayed, "Dear God, Help! I'm going down the tubes here." I didn't think God could or would answer my prayer. But He did.

"In my distress I called to the Lord;
I cried to my God for help.
He parted the heavens and came down."
Psalm 18:6, 9

He let me hit bottom. The occasion was another pharmaceutical trip—this time to Hawaii. The men had meetings in the mornings and the wives were free to do as they pleased all day.

Someone told me the hotel was known for their Bloody Marys, and I had two the first morning. Since people who drink like to be with other people who do, I found the wives I knew would drink with me and we had leisurely lunches together. At night there was a hospitality suite where the couples could party and have cocktails before going to a dinner where wine was also served. I thought I was having a wonderful time.

The next morning, I had no idea if I'd taken my contacts out the night before, or if they were still in my eyes. When I found them and looked out the window, I saw some of the ladies playing tennis. I wondered how they could do that when I felt so lousy.

As the night to fly home drew near, I worried that I might be sick if I drank too much and embarrass myself on the plane. I tried to cut back on my alcohol consumption before we left and thankfully, I survived the flight.

The excessive drinking on the trip, however, had caused me to become so frightened that when we arrived home and the idea came into my head to quit drinking for one day, I was receptive to it (I didn't know the idea was from God—I figured that out later). Day after day the idea was there along with the ability to do it. I kept thinking, "I don't know how this is possible, but I'll take it." With God relegated to last place in my life, I even forgot I'd prayed the prayer for help!

Three days after the trip we packed the car to spend a long Thanksgiving weekend at Charlie's parents' home. We always brought our own alcohol because his parents didn't drink. Charlie asked me what wine I wanted to bring, and I said I was taking a break from drinking, so I didn't want to take any. As we were driving, I thought to myself that I could go to the store if I needed wine.

Charlie's mom always put the turkey in the oven to cook slowly the night before Thanksgiving. I was shocked when I woke up the next morning and the aroma from the turkey smelled delicious! I remembered being nauseous other years when I woke up to that smell.

My break from drinking continued, and after a month I felt better than I'd felt in years. In January, a friend invited me to a Bible study. I'd been invited before but always had an excuse not to attend. It's funny that my impression of people who went to a Bible study or a Bible church was that they were missing out on life. Little did I know what most of them had was an inner peace, a kind of joy that was absent from my life, and a feeling of security even when facing the storms of life.

Since I didn't have hangovers anymore, I decided I would go once to the Bible study, and then if anyone asked me again, I'd be able to say that "it wasn't my bag." I was in the back seat of the car and the two girls in the front kept talking about "the Lord" this and "the Lord" that, all the way to the church.

I thought to myself, "Turn it off! If I ever do believe like they do, I won't talk about it!"

I filled out the registration card at Bible Study Fellowship even though I really didn't plan to come back. Then the lady talking to newcomers said, "People wonder why so many women gather faithfully every week to study the Bible." But she didn't tell us why! That was enough to make me take the homework questions, find the Bible I'd received for confirmation, and open it.

The lesson was Matthew, chapter 13, and when I got to verse 22, I suddenly realized the words were true and were describing me personally. I felt that God was right there showing me what I had never seen before—my sin that needed to be forgiven.

"'The one who received the seed that fell among the thorns
is the man who hears the word,
but the worries of this life
and the deceitfulness of wealth choke it,
making it unfruitful.'"
Matthew 13:22

Jesus said those words, and it was clear He was talking about me. I knew Jesus died for the sin of the world; I just didn't know that meant me. I was shocked when I saw I had choked God out my life because, in my pride, I thought I knew better than He did how my life should be lived.

At that moment, the dryer bell rang. I got up from reading the Bible, took the things from the dryer, put them on the bed and started folding clothes. There were full-length mirrors on the closet doors in the bedroom, and as I was thinking about the fact that my sins had choked God out of my life, I looked in the mirror and saw myself as the showy, worldly woman I always thought I wanted to be, except I was a haughty sham. My heart started to pound with panic as I realized I'd been chasing all the wrong things, and I didn't want to be that person anymore!

> *"'Come now, let us reason together," says the Lord.*
> *"Though your sins are like scarlet,*
> *they shall be white as snow.'"*
> Isaiah 1:18

I agreed with God that my sins were many, and in the same instant I knew my sins were gone. Washed away. Jesus became my Savior right then and there. I knew immediately that I belonged to God and would go to heaven—not because I deserved to, but the exact opposite: I didn't deserve to. Jesus, however, died for me, and mercifully said, "I forgive you; I'll take you."

The relief I felt was wonderful. I was ecstatic, to put it mildly, and I could think of nothing else. I was no longer a wreck because now my mind was consumed with wanting to know what this new life was all about. Wow! God was no longer in last place in my heart and in my mind. He was in first place and it felt right and good.

To this day, I will never get over the difference between plowing through life on my own and walking calmly with the One I can trust who knows the best way. Jesus is the answer.

> *"Teach me your way, O Lord,*
> *and I will walk in your truth;*
> *give me an undivided heart,*
> *that I may fear your name.*
> *I will praise you, O Lord my God,*
> *with all my heart;*
> *I will glorify your name forever.*
> *For great is your love toward me;*
> *you have delivered me from the depths of the grave."*
> Psalm 86:11-13

> *"A Christian is one who trusts in the wits and wisdom of God, and not his own wits."*[1]
> ~ Oswald Chambers ~

Betty

She just wanted to be somebody special.
Always worried what others thought.
Never wondered what God thought.
Fashion magazine said you can never be
too thin, too tan, or too rich.
Then I'll be somebody, she told herself.

Marriage and family
and "things" came her way.
Yet she searched for something elusive
to satisfy the void.
Attended church for looks…heart not in it.
Prayed repetitious prayers with a wandering mind.
Worries never left.

Started drinking every day pretending all was well.
Social butterfly with wine…depressed without.
Drank more to cope.

Sank to new depths in a mental prison with no escape.
Wished she wouldn't drink.
Couldn't stop.

Walking on thin ice...drowning emotionally.
Would she go to heaven if she slit her wrists and died?
"Dear God, help!"
"I'm going down the tubes here."
Didn't think He'd answer...didn't think He could.

Stopped drinking one day.
Continued to stop, day after day,
wondering how could this be?
Forgot she prayed the prayer asking for help.

Invited to Bible study.
Found out Jesus is God,
sent to die on the cross to pay for her sins.
She believed and was rescued.
The weight of addiction lifted for good.
Eternal life was hers.

God answered her prayer!
Happiest day of her life!
Finally, she's somebody special:
God's own child, with blessings galore.
Life is always better now, belonging to Jesus.
Guaranteed security anyone can have,
just for believing He is Lord.

New and Exciting

Can you imagine the incredible difference between waking up every day under a cloud of doom with a hangover headache and a stomach full of knots to waking up every day with a clear mind and the realization that everything is new and exciting?

When you go from a life of watching daytime television and playing solitaire because you don't feel good enough to do anything else, to being happy to see your children's faces in the morning while noticing that the view out the window is stunningly picturesque—it is a thrilling change!

Suddenly I woke up smiling, looking forward to what the day would hold and living in the "now" instead of in a "fake" world. That's what having Jesus in your life can do. What a gift!

I couldn't wait to go back to the Bible study. I had the homework all finished in two days and wanted more homework. I didn't tell anybody right away that I was a new Christian for fear they would ask me something I didn't know. I just sat there and soaked it all in, thrilled to listen and learn. I wanted to know everything there was to know about God!

They told me that when Jesus comes into your life, the Holy Spirit comes into your heart. He will be your Counselor, the Bible says. That was news to me, and I was so innocent that I came home thinking if that was true, He wouldn't want to be watching all of the stuff I was watching on television. And He confirmed it when I went to turn on the television. He didn't appear in person or talk out loud, but in my mind, I heard Him tell me quietly but clearly not to watch TV. I knew it was God talking to me, and surprisingly, instead of thinking, "But I want to watch TV," I thought, "Hmm, well, OK."

Then I opened a cupboard door and reached for my favorite deck of cards which had beautiful pictures on them— flowers along a canal in Venice, Italy. Seeing the scenes on the cards had always given me a brief moment of calmness, remembering a happier time before I gave alcohol control of my life. Again, in my mind I heard the Holy Spirit say, "No more solitaire." I didn't know it then, but thanks to the

Holy Spirit I would now be experiencing a peacefulness and a joy I'd never known before—just for the asking—no glass of wine, TV, or deck of cards necessary.

Eliminating daytime television and solitaire surely did free up my time for worthy pursuits! Almost immediately somebody told me about Christian programming on the radio. I didn't know there was such a thing! Now God poured into me from all of the wonderful speakers on the Chicago Moody Bible station—pastors such as Charles Stanley and Chuck Swindoll. I needed to know how Christians think, and between the Bible itself and the Bible teachers on the radio I learned in a hurry. From my formerly wasted days to "God's theology school," I was an eager student.

"Open my eyes that I may see
wonderful things in your law."
Psalm 119:18

"When your words came, I ate them;
they were my joy and my heart's delight,
for I bear your name, O Lord God Almighty."
Jeremiah 15:16

Extravagant Love

One of the first verses I read in the Bible was spoken by Jesus: "'Love the Lord your God with all your heart and with all your soul and with all your mind. This is the first and greatest commandment'" (Matthew 22:37-38).

I believed God was real, but I didn't know why I should love Him. Besides, I needed someone to love me! It was too embarrassing to ask anybody how to love God, so I very sincerely asked God to please tell me.

How gracious our God is! He showed me the verses that said He loved me first! Nothing could separate me from His love! This made a huge impact on me. It placed a value on me I never had before. It was the confidence builder I needed; I had worth in God's eyes. He loved me so much that he gave His only begotten Son for me. I could hardly believe it—Jesus died for me!

> *"'For God so loved the world*
> *that he gave his one and only son,*
> *that whoever believes in him shall not perish*
> *but have eternal life.'"*
> John 3:16

When someone loves you enough to give His life for you while you're running away from Him in pursuit of everything but Him, the word "crazy" comes to mind. God's love is outlandish. We don't deserve it; He gives it anyway. When I finally believed Jesus is the Savior of the world (and that meant me), I was covered with a love I'd never known before. And I know that love will carry me into eternity.

Everybody wants to matter to somebody. We long to be loved so much that we would never have a second thought about whether that love would be true, rock solid and always there. Can there be such a thing? Yes! Jesus' love is like that. Nothing can come between Him and the one He loves. That's why I love the Lord my God with all my heart!

> *"We love because He first loved us."*
> 1 John 4:19

> *"'I have loved you with an everlasting love;*
> *I have drawn you with loving kindness.'"*
> Jeremiah 31:3

"'...in all these things we are more than conquerors,
through him who loved us.
For I am convinced that neither death nor life,
neither angels nor demons,
neither the present nor the future, nor any powers,
neither height nor depth,
nor anything else in all creation,
will be able to separate us from the love of God
that is in Christ Jesus our Lord.'"
Romans 8:37

God Speaks

As I continued going to Bible Study Fellowship classes, I found out why people study the Bible. It's a fascinating book. It's not what man thinks about God; it's what God thinks about man. God outlines how to live a successful, rewarding life, and how to have peace and joy even amidst various troubles. The Bible is full of practical principles that work. A well-known theologian named Charles Haddon Spurgeon once said "A Bible that is falling apart generally is possessed by a person who is not."

Many people don't know this, but God does talk. He speaks through His Word. He writes that His Word is flawless, alive, active, and sharper than a two-edged sword. He says it's a hammer that breaks a rock in two. If a person's heart and mind are as hard as a rock, God's Word can crack that solid block.

He can cause what He has written to jump off the page and strike you in a way that leaves no doubt He's talking to you. When I accepted the fact that He loved me and gave His only begotten Son for my life, everything He wrote and said became life giving truth and indispensable wisdom. Hooray! If you want to hear from God when you read the Bible, be sure to listen. He says, "Be still and know that I am God"

(Psalm 46:10). Also, pray before reading and accept the Word of God, "...not as the word of men, but as it actually is, the Word of God, which is at work in you who believe" (1Thessalonians 2:13). Pray that He will open your eyes to see wonderful things in His word. Then read, listen, and believe.

"'I, the Lord, speak the truth;
I declare what is right.'"
Isaiah 45:19

Only God

I was 46 years old when I first believed in Jesus and started studying the Bible. Our boys were teenagers and definitely not interested in talking about God, let alone Jesus. They had to be bribed to go to church.

One day while reading in the book of Genesis (the first book in the Bible), I stopped and closed my eyes to pray. I asked God, "Will my sons ever believe?"

When I opened my eyes, I read the words, "'So shall your offspring be'" (Genesis 15:5). Wow, an immediate answer. I was thrilled! At different times over the next 10 years, both sons trusted Christ as their Savior and Lord. My husband did, too.

Only God could take a family that was falling apart and give each member a new life of purpose, peace, and joy. One-by-one we discovered why knowing Jesus is the answer to our often-difficult lives.

"This is what the Lord says,
he who made the earth, the Lord who formed it
and established it—the Lord is his name:
'Call to me and I will answer you and tell you
great and unsearchable things you do not know.'"
Jeremiah 33:2-3

"...listen to His voice, and hold fast to Him.
For the Lord is your life..."
Deuteronomy 30:20

"'Speak, Lord, for your servant is listening.'"
1 Samuel 3:9-10

CHAPTER 3

God Pursues an Agnostic

Have you ever tried to make a teenager believe something he doesn't want to believe? For instance, you can make him go to church, but you cannot make him believe in God. Only God can do that—and how He does it is always fascinating.

I was a brand-new Christian when our oldest son Steve was a senior in high school. He went off to college saying he was an agnostic. I had no idea what God was capable of doing in his life!

God Seeking Steve

When I quit drinking and started reading the Bible, listening to Christian radio, and talking about God, my family noticed. I overheard, "What happened to mom? She's different."

Steve, on his weekends home from college, decided to make it his mission to talk me out of my new faith. I had only been attending Bible study for five months, so my Bible knowledge was limited. Yet, I began to see a pattern unfold. Every Tuesday I would learn something at Bible study that, remarkably, would be the answer to Steve's questions on Saturday morning.

Of course, he didn't see it that way. We would discuss, and he would argue. Once, he even told me I didn't argue right, left the house and slammed the door! Neither of us realized that God had begun pursuing Steve, and Steve was resisting.

Over the next four years, I watched as God pursued, and Steve inquired. It's an interesting fact that God says His Word (the Bible) is alive. He calls it "God-breathed." He also says it won't return to Him void but will accomplish the purpose for which He wrote it.

> *"All Scripture is God-breathed*
> *and is useful for teaching,*
> *rebuking, correcting,*
> *and training in righteousness,*
> *that the man of God*
> *may be thoroughly equipped*
> *for every good work."*
> 2 Timothy 3:16-17

> *"'...so is my word that goes out from my mouth:*
> *It will not return to me empty,*
> *but will accomplish what I desire*
> *and achieve the purpose for which I sent it.'"*
> Isaiah 55:11

> *"For the Word of God is living and active.*
> *Sharper than any double-edged sword,*
> *it penetrates even to dividing soul and spirit,*
> *joints and marrow;*
> *It judges the thoughts and attitudes of the heart."*
> Hebrews 4:12

God Engineers Circumstances

There were several steps along the way of Steve's journey to God. During his first year away at college, he called and told me he had signed up for a program about God and astronomy at the University of Wisconsin, which is home to the Washburn Observatory and the WIYN telescope. Steve had always been interested in astronomy. I didn't tell him, but I called the University to find out who was sponsoring the program to see if it was a new age or an evangelical group. It was Campus Crusade for Christ (CRU) and Intervarsity Christian Fellowship. Whew!

Afterwards, he called to say he enjoyed the program and had signed a card "to know more." He said a student followed up and came to his dorm room. His next comment still makes me smile. He said, "Well, mom, he wasn't a dork! He was a nice guy who believes like you do, and he explained things and then asked me if I wanted to believe like that. I said, 'No, I'm not ready yet!'"

My Bible study leader told me his saying he wasn't ready yet was a good sign because it showed that Steve was beginning to discern the truth about who Jesus is.

Another step along the way seemed to completely backfire. Steve was home for the summer, and I convinced him to attend a church service with me at a local summer Bible conference. Since my husband was golfing and our younger son wasn't home, the two of us went to hear a well-known guest preacher. Driving back, I was on cloud nine because Steve had heard such a wonderful message, but he quickly dispelled my hopes saying he didn't like anything the man said.

Many times, when God is pursuing, the recipient takes a step forward, then two steps back. Since Steve was a philosophy major, I gave him a copy of the book Mere Christianity, by C. S. Lewis, an atheist who converted to

Christianity and has been described as one of the intellectual giants of the 20th century. I knew Steve would be a "tough sell," but I honestly thought he'd agree it was interesting. He read it, said he didn't like it, and didn't agree with it.

But God continued to hound him. By this time, Steve had transferred to the University of Michigan and was now a senior. He signed up for a class about Jesus and the Gospels. I was thrilled when he called home and said he needed a Bible! He was peeved with me for engraving his name on the cover. The class was taught from a secular point of view (I saw the syllabus). Nevertheless, because God's word is like a hammer that breaks a rock in pieces, reading it caused Steve's wall of resistance to crack just a bit. Yet when I invited him to go to church, he immediately strengthened his resolve saying, "I'm not going, and don't ask me again!"

A few months later, something earthshaking happened. Steve met Jesus.

"But the plans of the Lord stand firm forever,
the purposes of his heart through all generations."
Psalm 33:11

Christian

Steve is now an attorney, having established his own firm, Nance and Simpson, LLP, in Houston, Texas. He and his wife Jody and their three children attend Second Baptist Church. In his own words (written many years ago), this is how Steve became a believer in Jesus Christ:

"Growing up, I was a rebel, a partier, and a bit of a womanizer. I was even arrested three different times—all alcohol related. But my whole world was turned upside down on October 2, 1993, the day I became a Christian.

What being a Christian really means is having a time when you humbled yourself before God and accepted his son, Jesus Christ, as the boss of your life. Before, I knew about Jesus with my mind, but I never knew Him with my heart. In fact, I rejected Him. As a philosophy major at the University of Michigan, I was agnostic. I had lots of logical, philosophical, and scientific objections to faith. And I had no idea I even needed God. For many of us (myself included), you don't realize that God is all you need until God is all you have.

"While in the midst of a relationship crisis, I nearly overdosed on mushrooms and almost died. Physically I'm not sure how close I came to dying, but I can tell you that I was 100 percent sure in my own mind that I was going to die that day. I also knew, beyond a shadow of a doubt, that if and when I died, I was going to hell. I can't explain how I knew it, but I did. There is no fear quite like it. It was as real as it gets. I knew that was not what I wanted, and so having nowhere else to turn, I cried out to God for help. And He came to my rescue!"

"That day, I confessed myself a sinner before the Almighty Living God, turned away from my sin and asked Jesus Christ to be the Savior and Lord of my life. For me, Proverbs 1:7 was right on: the fear of God was the beginning of all wisdom. Biblical fear of God is simply knowing who God is and knowing who you are. He is the creator of the universe—the one who knitted you together in your mother's womb and who knows everything about you—including the number of hairs on your head. Knowing this truth for the first time blew me away. It was a bit scary at first. I had never really understood the reality of God or of heaven and hell before and that it was serious business."

"That day I prayed a prayer for the first time. I prayed that Jesus Christ would come into my life and save me. He came into my life at that very moment, and I have been a different person ever since. I was literally born again that day. I never knew what that meant until then, but Jesus was right when he said that no one can see the kingdom of God unless he is born again (John 3:3). I didn't understand much of what I was doing then or how it all worked, but that's one of the great things about faith—it doesn't matter how much faith you have it only matters who your faith is in. What's critical is understanding that you cannot earn your way into heaven. It doesn't work like that. Salvation is a gift. It is by God's grace alone that we are saved (Ephesians 2:8-9). You have to come to God exactly how you are—garbage and all."

"Now, years later, I can look back and chart my spiritual growth and understanding of the good news of Jesus. It was and is the most important thing that has ever happened or ever will happen to me. It is a question every person needs to answer for himself. "Who is Jesus?" is the most important question because it has eternal consequences. You will find that there are only three possible answers: Jesus is (1) Lord, (2) liar, or (3) lunatic. He said He was God, and that no one comes to the Father but by Him. If He was telling the truth, the first answer is correct. The truth is that Jesus Christ was a real person who lived and walked on the earth in Israel. He was the son of God—conceived by the Holy Spirit, and He died on Calvary—on the cross—as a willing sacrifice to pay the price for sin. For Steve Simpson's sin, for Mother Teresa's sin, and for your sin. We are all the same. He took our place on that cross—so that we don't have to experience spiritual death ourselves.

What I never realized before was how personal God's provision through Jesus is. Jesus died for me and for you, and we can know and experience Him. We just have to seek Him. What's weird is that even the desire to seek Him is a gift from God—so that no one can boast.

Becoming a believer does not mean all my problems were fixed. But what I have now that I never had before is an anchor in life—a rock. I know I will never be alone no matter what because Jesus loves me, and He will never forsake me.

This is peace with God.

> *"For it is by grace you have been saved, through*
> *faith—and this not from yourselves,*
> *it is the gift of God—*
> *not by works, so that no one can boast."*
> Ephesians 2:8-9

Simply Wonderful

And now there were two of us in my family who believed in Jesus. God kept His promise and I couldn't stop thanking Him. I couldn't stop smiling, either!

It's a little strange, but before Bible study I don't remember ever hearing the term "born again" explained in church. I did hear acquaintances use the phrase and it made me very uncomfortable. Without even knowing why, somehow it signified a big commitment to Jesus that I hoped was unnecessary. I thought anyone who said they were a "born again" Christian was a fanatic. Yet on the other hand, I figured whatever it meant, maybe I was "it" simply because I had gone to church most of my life.

It is mind boggling to me now when I remember the day Jesus came into my heart, forgave my sin, and I felt the relief of belonging to Him. I suddenly thought, "I'll bet this is what being born again means!" I went from almost gagging at the term to being totally excited about it.

The very next day, I found a Christian bookstore and asked if they had a book that explained the term "born again." They gave me Peace with God by Billy Graham. I took it home and read it cover to cover, all the while thinking, "Yay, this is me!" I recommend this book for anyone who has questions like I did.

Being born again happens when you believe in Jesus. He forgives your sins, takes your old life and gives you His righteousness in exchange. You become a new person and your new life never ends. I found out it's nothing to be afraid of because it's simply wonderful!

> "'You should not be surprised at my saying,
> 'You must be born again.'"
> John 3:7

> "Therefore, if anyone is in Christ, he is a new creation;
> the old has gone, the new has come!
> All this is from God, who reconciled us
> to himself through Christ."
> 2 Corinthians 5:17-18

Choose Jesus

An awesome fact is our God, the God of the Bible, is the only God who desires a relationship with the people He created. The Bible says He sent His son Jesus to rescue us from our stiff-necked independence, and He did it because He loved us before we ever thought about loving Him.

After telling a dear friend about my faith, she said she didn't like my way of believing—that Jesus is the only way a person can go to heaven. She said she liked her way better—believing God grades on a curve, and good people go to heaven and bad people don't. I told her believing in Jesus isn't my way, it's God's way.

It is tempting to believe there are other ways to God, all easier than believing in Jesus, until you find out all other routes are man-made and based on earning your way by being good more than being bad. If that were true, it'd be frightening because how would you know you were good enough, except in your own estimation? The Bible clearly says no one is good enough. All have sinned.

With Jesus, there's no guesswork! Believe He died on the cross for your sins and ask Him into your life. Peace will flood your heart.

"For all have sinned and fall short of the glory of God..."
Romans 3:23

"Salvation is found in no one else,
for there is no other name under heaven given to men
by which we must be saved."
Acts 4:12

Steve's Journey

God was knocking on Steve's door,
but he didn't know it, and he didn't care.
Mostly he was irritated.
How could Mom believe that stuff the Bible said?

Off to college he went, thinking life was an illusion.
Mom said, "If you ask God, He will prove Himself."
"Well I'm not asking," Steve said.
God kept pursuing, and Steve kept resisting.
Mom kept praying.

Then a personal crisis rocked Steve's illusory world.
To sooth his distress, he overdosed on mushrooms.
Thought he was dying...finally called for help.
"God, if you're real please give me another chance."
The rescuer came in person just for him.
Jesus was His Name.

Steve's life changed forever that night.
Now he believes beyond a shadow of a doubt:
Jesus is Lord.

He tells his friends, "Don't wait!
Believe Jesus died for your sins,
like He did for mine.
Believe He loves you, because He does.
And He will save you, if you ask."

Chapter 4

God Saves a Marriage and a Husband

Why do you think love is so difficult to maintain? I think it's because of selfishness. At least it was in my case—I was selfish. Whether you are married, divorced, or single, there are things you and I can apply to our relationships with a spouse, a child, a friend, and others to maintain the love. These things are straight out of the Bible and are love-building-blocks instead of love-destroying-chisels.

 God has a lot to say about nourishing the love you and I have for others. My favorite life-transforming statement of God's is this: "Love never fails" (1 Corinthians 13:8).

When you and I respond in love, no matter who we face or what the circumstances are, we are doing what God wants us to do. It isn't easy, but God did set the example—He loved us when we were unlovable (Romans 5:8). That's why He is pleased, and you and I are blessed when we give love as a first response.

While I know this now, during the first 20 years of marriage, I wasn't very good at it!

Wingtips

Now that God was in our household, I was anxious to see what He would do next. I asked in prayer, and when He told me, I balked! It seemed an impossibility. God wanted me to love my husband, Charlie, unconditionally.

I said, "I can't. He has too many faults."

God has a prickly way of making His points clear. He reminded me that He loves me, and I also have "too many faults!" At that time, my new faith was fresh and childlike, and I very sincerely and humbly said to God, "Then will you please just make me love him?"

At this point in our marriage I wasn't sure Charlie really loved me anymore. I had a mental list of all the things he did or didn't do that I kept to myself because he and I couldn't discuss anything without me ending up in tears. It seemed we were going through our marriage with no real love involved. I never thought about leaving him, though, because I didn't want to be a single mother with two young boys.

Now, many years later, Charlie affectionately calls this story, "My husband was an idiot!" But I tell him, no; we were both idiots—just two people trying to stay married having no idea God had a plan for husbands and wives to fall in love and stay in love.

God doesn't ask us to do something without giving instructions and the ability to do it. Almost immediately I heard on Christian radio about a book by the late Ed Wheat, M.D., called Love Life for Every Married Couple. In the introduction to the book, Dr. Wheat wrote that he began his practice as a family physician, but soon discovered many problems he was asked to treat could not be resolved medically. He was totally unfamiliar with the Bible, but God used a patient of his to introduce him to the Lord Jesus Christ. Dr. Wheat, then poured himself into learning what the Word of God had to say about being a husband and father. He became a Bible-based marriage counselor, a certified sex therapist, and an author of many books on these topics.

God used one chapter in Dr. Wheat's book about married love to transform Charlie's and my marriage. The chapter was called "Prescription for a Superb Marriage."

Of course, being a brand-new Christian, I thought that my husband was the only one who needed to change—certainly not me! You can probably guess that God started working on me first. He showed me that I never gave any thought to my husband and what would please him. My children were far more important to me. In fact, they were all I thought about besides myself. What an eye opener to discover that God should come first in our lives, our spouses are next—that was a real shock to me—and then our children.

Once I got the order straight, God gave me four principles from that one chapter in Dr. Wheat's book as a recipe for a superb marriage. I took God seriously and made a real effort to put those principles into practice. In fact, I was fired up about it, excited to see what God would do. I told Charlie, "I'm going to start working on our marriage, and you don't have to do anything!"

He said, "Well, OK."

He didn't know God was behind this, and I didn't tell him because at that time he was quite leery of my new faith. I just said I was reading a book and things were going to get better for us.

The first principle Dr. Wheat described was "Blessing." A Christian wife can be a blessing to her husband even when he doesn't deserve it. Wives can have power from God's Holy Spirit to stop arguments and kill bitterness with kind words. Thoughtful, gracious words should be our first response.

Is this easy? NO! Without God's supernatural strength it would be impossible.

Is it worth it? YES!

Charlie and I used to play the blame game. If he wouldn't do something for me, then I wouldn't do something for him. And then we'd blame each other for our unhappiness about the situation.

One day Charlie was giving me what I called a "corrective interview." I so badly wanted to respond in the old way, with accusations and blame, but I stepped into the next room for a brief moment and asked God, "This is a test, isn't it? Please don't let me blow it."

God answered. I kept my mouth shut for the rest of the corrective interview. My silence allowed God to work behind the scenes and make things better.

Following that first lesson of letting God be the leader and me doing what He told me to do, I tackled Dr. Wheat's next principle which was called "Edifying." The advice was to build up my husband and cheer him on by thinking about the things I found attractive about him. This is hard to do when the mind draws a blank!

There's a verse in the Bible that says, "If there's anything excellent or praiseworthy, let your mind dwell on these things" (Philippians 4:8). I tried to remember what attracted me to Charlie in the first place, and all I could think of (honestly) was his pair of wingtip shoes. I thought he looked fantastic in them! So, I started telling him how handsome he looked in a suit and tie and wingtips as he left for work. I expected nothing from Charlie in return—my mission was just to be complimentary and positive. He began to look better and better to me! And that was only the beginning of what God was accomplishing.

The bottom line of this lesson is to always build up—never tear down. Your mate becomes the person you tell him he or she is. This works with children and friends, too!

Dr. Wheat's step number three was about "Sharing." All I had to do was listen to Charlie and be aware of moments that could become special times together. The first few years I was a Christian, instead of spending time in the evenings with my husband, I was either studying the Bible in another room, or listening to Christian radio, while he watched TV. One day he said to me, "Something's come between us. It's your Bible study!" Wow—a red flag went up—I knew that wasn't right. I decided right then to watch TV with him at night, just so we could be together.

The fourth and last principle from that chapter in Love Life for Every Married Couple was "Touching." Dr. Wheat wrote: "Experts say that our extreme preoccupation with sex today actually shows a very deep need for the warmth and reassurance of nonsexual touching. A tender touch tells us we are cared for. It can calm our fears, soothe pain, be comforting, and provide emotional security. It's a primary way of communicating with the one you love." Then Dr. Wheat listed 25 suggestions for physical closeness and touching in his book.

Charlie and I typically did not hold hands, or sit close to each other, or anything else on the list. The first time I tried to implement this principle I put my arms around Charlie from behind as he was standing in front of the TV. He pulled away and said, "What'd I do now?" That tells you it felt awkward to both of us, and he had no idea I was trying to give him a hug. He thought I was going to accuse him of something. The good news is that we have since discovered how loving a casual touch can be!

After several months of God working on both of us, our marriage was noticeably different. One morning as Charlie was leaving for work and saw me doing my Bible study, he said to me, "I don't know what you're reading in that Bible but keep on reading it!" I did. We fell in love all over again, and now I have a long list of things I love about my husband!

The four principles Dr. Wheat used in his book, **B**lessing, **E**difying, **S**haring, and **T**ouching spell out the word **BEST**. With these four principles he said that your goal to create the BEST marriage, is possible.2

*"What, then, shall we say in response to this?
If God is for us, who can be against us?"*
Romans 8:31

*"...whatever is true, whatever is noble,
whatever is right, whatever is pure, whatever is lovely,
whatever is admirable—
if anything is excellent or praiseworthy—
think about such things...put it into practice.
And the God of peace will be with you."*
Philippians 4:8-9

Trailer Hitch

You may think you should occasionally tell God what to do. We've probably all done it. During my months of "God's Marriage Repair Clinic," I occasionally got off the track, messed up, and then tried to dictate to God. I had trouble trusting Him to do what He knew was best.

One day Charlie asked me to be home at 5 o'clock with my car because it had a trailer hitch. He needed it to take our ski boat for winter storage.

I completely forgot, mainly because I'd been selfish for so long that I only thought about myself and the kids, not my husband and his requests.

There were no cell phones then, so by the time he figured out where I might be and called me at my sister's house, he let me know how very unhappy he was. I had made plans with my sister to take my mom and dad to a support group for caregivers of Alzheimer's patients (for my dad) that evening. It sounds noble, but nevertheless, I hadn't thought to call Charlie at work to tell him.

When we met halfway between her house and ours to trade cars, Charlie commented about the inconvenience I'd created for him. I was in tears while driving back to attend the support group with my mom.

On the way home that evening, I was discussing with God how "put out" I was. I told God I thought I should tell Charlie that he shouldn't say things that made me cry as I was now a child of God and it was unacceptable! God made it clear to me that I needed to take my hands off the problem and zip my mouth shut. I argued with God about it, but when I got home, I decided to try it God's way ...except I went overboard and didn't speak to Charlie at all!

Later that night, I opened a devotional book, still stewing about why I couldn't tell Charlie off, and my eyes fell on the phrase "it matters for eternity." Suddenly I knew God's reason, and it was a big deal! Since my goal was for our whole family to be in heaven together forever, this meant God wanted me to show Charlie the love and forgiveness that Jesus gave to me, not my ugly "I'm mad at you" attitude. If I could do this, then Charlie would want to say "yes" to Jesus, too.

Even with such incredible truth from God, I was still mad at Charlie and I chose to sleep in the guest bedroom that night (It took years for me to learn that loving others is the only way to show them who Jesus is).

In the morning I got up as Charlie was leaving for work. Unbeknownst to me, God had touched Charlie's heart overnight. He put his arms around me and for the first time in our married lives, he said, "I'm sorry." Of course, that made me cry happy tears!

Then he added, "I don't know why I'm the one saying I'm sorry when you're the one who forgot to bring the car with the trailer hitch home!" I was so happy he said he was sorry I wasn't even fazed by the extra comment, because God had just proven to me that obeying God pays off big time.

And that was only the very beginning of what God has done in Charlie's and my marriage and in our lives!

"Clothe yourselves with compassion, kindness,
humility, gentleness, and patience.
Bear with each other and forgive whatever grievances
you may have against one another.
Forgive as the Lord forgave you.
And over all these virtues put on love,
which binds them all together in perfect unity."
Colossians 3:12-14

"Trust in the Lord with all your heart and
lean not on your own understanding;
in all your ways acknowledge Him,
and He will make your paths straight."
Proverbs 3:5-6

God's Way is Best

It's easy to say, "I believe in God." But can you say you believe God? Believe what He says in His Word? It will save a lot of time agonizing over life's problems if you take

God at his Word. There are so many things in life that only God can do—and that's why they are called miracles. I'd been given God's formula for a superb marriage, yet I got off the track and had to re-learn the invaluable truth that God's way is best!

What many people forget is that they're not perfect! When Charlie read this portion of the book, he said (with a big grin on his face) that he thought I should add a footnote saying this is my side of the story, not his! And he's right; I know there are still times when I don't live up to his expectations.

He and I are opposites. He's a 'type A,' very capable person who knows what to do and gets it done. He's outgoing, likable, and is never late. I am an artistic introvert who loses all track of time and hates to be on a schedule of any kind. He's neat and sees every cobweb; I'm unorganized, messy, and live with stacks of paper on the counters. The truth is, now that we're in love again, I wish I was more like him!

The trailer hitch story certainly wasn't the only time I didn't take God at his Word. I had a hard time giving up the "silent treatment," and carrying a grudge. Once I was so mad at Charlie, I even told God to "Come and get me! I don't want to be here anymore!"

That was rash, and childish, but God's gracious answer proves we can be real and honest with Him. I'll never forget what He said in that moment: "Do you want to miss what I'm going to do in your husband's life?"

I was in the guest bedroom (again!) and when God said that, I sat straight up in bed and confessed, "I never thought of that! I'm so sorry, God. I really don't want to miss anything!"

Now, years later, I can tell you God was right. He delivered. I'm so glad I did it His way (with a few missteps), and not my way. Charlie is a wonderful man who makes me feel special every day. I'm crazy about him and the love we share is something I never would have believed possible. We've learned to look at and appreciate the good things about each other and to truly care for each other. A miracle has taken place!

"As for God, his way is perfect;
the word of the Lord is flawless."
2 Samuel 22:31

"You are the God who performs miracles;
you display your power among the peoples."
Psalm 77:14

Church

After I'd been going to Bible study for quite a while and had found it fascinating, I wondered if attending a Bible church would be just as interesting. There was a Bible church in our small town that others at Bible study liked, so one Sunday while Charlie was golfing, I went with a friend to the Bible church. The teaching was aimed at applying the truth of the Bible to our daily lives in a way that would help us to be more like Jesus. Besides that, it was a friendly church and the music was great.

It was spring or summer when I first visited the Bible church. From then on, Charlie and I fell into a pattern of going to his church together on Saturday night, and on Sunday morning, I went to the Bible church while he played golf. When cold weather arrived, we both went to our separate churches on Sunday morning and met for breakfast afterwards.

One year, at Christmastime, while Steve was home from law school and Matt from college, I asked Charlie if he would go to the Bible church for just two Sundays with the boys and me. Steve was now a Christian and attending a Bible teaching church near his law school, and I figured I could get Matt to go just because it was Christmas. It was nice to be in church as a family. After the New Year, when the boys were back in school, Charlie surprised me and decided he would continue going to the Bible church with me.

It has been such a blessing for our family that Jesus rescued me and then led all of us to Bible study groups and Bible teaching churches. Our lives have been enriched by finding out what the Bible is all about and what the truth means for each of us. We've discovered that living God's way fills all of the voids in life and answers most of the questions. I say "most" because we're never going to have all of the answers. Instead, God fills us with the unmistakably clear assurance that we can trust Him anyway because He loves us, and He has a divine plan. If we start to lose our faith, He gives us truth from the Bible to build it up again.

I would never want to go back to the way things were before Jesus, and neither would Charlie or the boys. It's not that we're sinless and perfect now—it's that we're forgiven. Jesus loves us and we're excited about following Him. That's a feeling of joy that can't be duplicated on earth in any other way. To think that God grabbed me first and then one-by-one the rest of my family still amazes me. We all resisted, not having any idea what we were missing. Now that we know, our goal is for others to know the same personalized love and forgiveness.

Tim Keller is the pastor of Redeemer Presbyterian Church in New York City, which is the church our younger son, Matt, and his wife, Rebecca, attended when they lived there. They enjoyed his messages so much they would listen to tapes of his sermons while walking to work and back. I love the way Tim Keller explains who Jesus is in this quote from his book, Making Sense of God.

"Jesus essentially says to us: I call you only to do those things you were created to do, and you will find therefore that my yoke is easy. I put on you the burden of following me, but I have already paid the price, so that when you fail you will be forgiven. I've taken off you the burdens that other people have. I've removed the burden of earning your own salvation through your striving and effort. I've removed the burden of guilt or shame for past failures. I've taken off the burden of having to prove yourself worthy of love. I am therefore the only Lord and master who, if you find me, will satisfy you, and, if you fail me, will forgive you."[3]

"'You will seek me and find me
when you seek me with all your heart.'"
Jeremiah 29:13

Priorities

This is Charlie's testimony, adapted from his September 2002 presentation at Gracespring Bible Church in Richland, Michigan:

"I have been blessed for many years, but for the first 56 I thought I was in control of my life and the events were of my doing, just plain lucky, or being in the right place at the right time. Many can probably relate to my story, for there's nothing in my life that has been particularly challenging or of any major consequence, besides having to overcome a lifelong stutter, and raising a spirited family. These I am sure are not National Enquirer stories."

"But, you know, sometimes it's not good when things are relatively easy for you and your life seems to not need anything—particularly Jesus. For me it was harder to recognize that it wasn't me who was in control of my life. I didn't think I needed anybody. But the Lord gradually worked on me to ask Jesus to forgive me and come into my life, as I saw that He was the one in control of it."

"What I remember most about my early religious childhood was the attention to rules and regulations—not so much the teaching of the Bible—surely not much about the salvation message, but the emphasis on living a good life and doing good deeds. I believe my family was, and continues to be, a loving family and very strong in supporting each other. My father's influence was mostly a quiet one consisting mainly of sports, instilling a good work ethic and having a 'never give up' attitude. These attributes he instilled in me can best be described in one word: competitive. This competitive drive did me well both in sports and in the business world. My mother was the driving force behind my early spiritual growth as a Catholic."

"After graduating from the University of Detroit I took a job with The Upjohn Company, from which I am now retired. I would characterize my business career as successful, both financially and professionally. I traveled extensively to more than 38 countries. As my career took off, which I pridefully believed was due to my competitive and self-reliant character, my spiritual and family life took a back seat. Basically, I thought I was pretty hot stuff."

"As I look back now at my priorities, after marriage and two children, they were career, friends, hobbies, family, and then God (and then only on Sundays). This, I am ashamed to say, is probably the order it took. I was more concerned with what other people thought of me and what I was doing than anything else. Pride and selfishness ruled my life. There was no doubt that I was the most important person in my life. I believed my sole purpose was to be the provider, but of material things, not the spiritual leader that God outlines so clearly in the Bible."

"What brought me to the Lord?"

"With my formal Catholic education and my mother's strong traditional Catholic upbringing, I brought a lot of baggage into this new relationship with God (Jesus) that my wife Betty was describing to me. Betty had asked Jesus into her life in January of 1989, many years before I started to get the message. In time, I allowed Betty to find another church. She went to her church and I continued to go to mine. It wasn't long before I thought this was ridiculous because I wasn't getting anything out of mine, and what I had known about hers, which by the way was Gracespring Bible Church (GBC), was that there was at least an entertainment factor due to the musical talent and worship music. That was good enough for me to attend."

"At GBC I soon found that the messages of the Bible were taught in practical and illuminating ways, and I became interested in learning more each week. I probably learned more in one of our pastor's messages than I did with all my educational credits in theology at the University of Detroit. The salvation message was given several times, if not every week. Eventually, my mind and heart became convinced that this was the truth and what I wanted was to belong to Jesus. The changes I had seen in both my wife and my oldest son were also a constant reminder of the power of God. Then it happened! One Sunday in October of 1998, I raised my hand to accept Jesus as my Lord and Savior."

"My life has been filled with blessings since. I thank God every day for my wonderful wife who is both my lover and my best friend, and for my two sons, of whom I am so proud, and now two wonderful daughters-in-law who I love and respect. All are believers, walking with the Lord in their lives. What could be better than that?"

"I consider myself still a work in progress as far as my walk with Jesus, but at least I'm on the same side of the street. Why do I say this? Let me describe an event that amplifies one of the weaknesses I still pray to Jesus about. Jesus teaches being generous, because whatever wealth we are blessed with is really His. We are to be good stewards and use these gifts to further His kingdom and His children, etc. I think God put Betty in my life to be a constant reminder to me of this principle. God allowed me to have some financial success and make the money and He gave me Betty to give it away."

"This became so clear to me once when Betty and I were in New York City visiting our son and daughter-in-law. We were riding the subway and a homeless woman walked through the subway car rattling a cup asking for change. Most people avoid these encounters, but I know Betty's heart goes out to people like this. I reached into my pocket for some change. Not having any, I looked for a dollar, but I had none. I looked at Betty and asked her for a dollar. She looked at me and put five dollars in the lady's hand and told her it was from God. The lady went off in a state of shock but kept looking back at us with a big grin. I really admire the gift of giving that the Lord has given Betty and it reminds me more and more each time we have such an experience of the love that Jesus has for all His children.

"Let me close by thanking you for your attention to my story, and by reminding you to revisit your priorities in life."

"Blessed is the man who trusts in the Lord,
whose confidence is in him."
Jeremiah 17:7

"Who, then, is the man that fears the Lord?
He will instruct him in the way chosen for him."
Psalm 25:12

CHAPTER 5

God's Plans, Our Detours

If there was a road map with real destinations such as Disasterville or Black Hole City, you would change course if you saw yourself headed in the wrong direction. At least, I hope you would.

I didn't.

I think there are a lot of people like me who either have no idea they're going down the wrong road—or if they suspect they are, don't know what to do about it.

Since I made a lot of wrong turns—to the point of being totally lost—I'd like to share with you some of the traps I ran into that didn't have warning signs like "Wrong Way" or "Dead End." You'll see that God's GPS—the Bible—leads to the life He has planned for you versus the temptations and detours you may lack discernment and wisdom to avoid.

God's Road Map

Do you read directions or try to figure out things on your own first? I tried to figure out life on my own, and from my testimony you can see how that worked out for me! I didn't know that God has a plan for each one of us to live an abundant and joy-filled life with Him at the helm (Jeremiah 29:11).

My church didn't spell that out to me, and I doubt I would have been interested anyway, since I had my own ideas from day one. You never would have guessed that I did because I was a wimp! But down deep, I was a stubborn wimp. I just didn't want anyone telling me what to do. Even God.

The Bible is God's wonderful road map for living life and anybody can use it. He outlines principles and details about how to be prosperous and successful. But, even now, some of us who really want to do it God's way struggle to follow His plan instead of our own. Either we don't think the blessings will be that great, or we don't think the consequences for ignoring God's map will be that bad. Plus, we tend to forget that if God asks us to refrain from something, it's to protect us from what would eventually lead to our downfall—even to crushing defeat, as in my case.

God says His way is best. Not only best, but perfect. So, how can you trust that His design will lead to the most fulfilling life possible? I heard on Christian radio that you can only trust someone you know. It's true with people and it's true with God. You can hear about God and what He's like, but only when you open your heart and get to know Him as the God who created you, knows you, loves you, and cares about every detail of your life, will you truly be able to trust His itinerary.

God is personally involved in your life and mine. He wants the best for you. Many times in the Bible, God says, "Do what is right and good in the sight of the Lord, so that it may go well with you," or "that you may enjoy long life," or "so that you will always be at the top, never at the bottom" (Deuteronomy 6:18, Deuteronomy 6:2, Deuteronomy 28:13). The Bible says to take every thought captive, (think about what you're doing), and make it line up with God's plumb line. His plumb line is straight and leads to righteousness—right living—that leads to a blessed life.

When you read the Bible and embrace God's plan with the Holy Spirit's help, your life will be flooded with joy and unstoppable blessings! You'll be able to smile even when the road is full of twists and turns, bumps and bruises, because His plan is guaranteed.

"Taste and see that the Lord is good..."
Psalm 34:8

"'Do not let this Book of the Law
depart from your mouth;
meditate on it day and night,
so that you may be careful to do everything written in it.
Then you will be prosperous and successful.
Have I not commanded you? Be strong and courageous.
Do not be terrified; do not be discouraged,
for the Lord your God will be with you
wherever you go.'"
Joshua 1:8-9

"Acknowledge and take to heart this day
that the Lord is God in heaven
above and on the earth below.
There is no other.
Keep his decrees and commands,
which I am giving you today,
so that it may go well with you
and your children after you..."
Deuteronomy 4:39-40

"Show me the way I should go,
for to you I entrust my life."
Psalm 143:8

Pouring Out My Heart

One day when I wasn't following God's map, I wrote to Him in my journal. I poured out my heart about circumstances I was trying to manipulate without success, and it was only making me more miserable. I was literally trying to do God's job and make changes in someone else's life using all the wrong tactics. Have you ever tried to take the place of God like that? It's a dead-end road. I was actually making matters worse and didn't know it.

Pouring out my heart on paper was good, though, because God very lovingly brought to my mind a verse asking me if I was pure and without sin (Proverbs 20:9). Yikes. Suddenly it became clear to me that I'm not without sin and if it weren't for Jesus, I'd be doomed. My "better than somebody else" attitude combined with thinking I knew what to do was the prideful problem. Not only that, my sin is clearly worse before God than another person's sin since my pride is on top of the list of things God hates the most (Proverbs 6:16-19).

I asked God to please forgive me for standing in the way and blocking progress. I asked Him to soften my heart and help me to genuinely love and encourage anyone I was hoping to influence. I told Him I needed help to place this particular situation securely into His hands and leave it there!

Then I thanked Him for reminding me that He is in charge of the results—not me! And a weight was lifted from my mind. What a relief!

"I am still confident of this:
I will see the goodness of the Lord
in the land of the living.
Wait for the Lord;
be strong and take heart and wait for the Lord."
Psalm 27:13-14

Potholes and Barricades

There's an old saying that has proven to be true again and again: Sin will take you further than you ever wanted to go, cost you more than you ever wanted to pay, and keep you longer than you ever wanted to stay. It's really not a laughing matter. It's a sobering reminder of the perils of the things some of us do—from lying and being discontent, to abuse of any kind, infidelity, financial dishonesty, and more. All sin ends up harming you, your loved ones, and others.

Since I am a poster child for having made some poor choices and experiencing the consequences, I'm proof that sin took me further, cost me more, and kept me longer than I ever imagined. The wine that started out to be enjoyable and soothing eventually betrayed and frightened me almost to death. I shriveled up like a leaf in autumn and my sin swept me away (Isaiah 64:6). When any of us aren't following God's design for whatever reason, (not interested, stubborn, selfish, angry, or tired), Satan is waiting in the wings, anxious to whisper that we should do our own thing and not worry about whether it's a good idea or not.

It's interesting to me that God cannot lie, and Satan cannot tell the truth! You and I have to decide who we're going to listen to. It should be an easy decision. But, for some strange reason, when you've been lied to for a long time, it's easier to believe the lies than the truth. Just remember that God holds the patent on truth.

"Submit yourselves, then, to God.
Resist the devil, and he will flee from you.
Come near to God and he will come near to you."
James 4:7-8

"'I, the Lord, speak the truth;
I declare what is right.'"
Isaiah 45:19

Sin will always be a barricade that separates you from God. The only way to reach God is through Jesus. He took your sin upon Himself and died on the cross to pay for it. Ask Him to forgive you and you'll be free from guilt and shame. Can there be any better news than God doing such an awesome thing that we didn't expect or deserve? (See Isaiah 64:3)

There's no greater gift.

"If we confess our sins,
he is faithful and just and will forgive us our sins
and purify us from all unrighteousness."
1 John 1:9

"He does not treat us as our sins deserve,
or repay us according to our iniquities.
For as high as the heavens are above the earth,
so great is his love for those who fear him;
as far as the east is from the west,
so far has he removed our transgressions from us."
Psalm 103:10-12

Sinking Sand

Go ahead, the voice said.
Just one time, or maybe two.
It's your life, do what you want.
No one can tell you not to.
Sounded so right...easy to believe.
But no one said lies will ruin you, as they soothe you.

Then, storm clouds appear.
The promise disintegrates, life unravels.
Lost in denial, delusion running wild.
Trying in vain to stay sane,
a plastered smile over a crumbling mess.
Just a made-up persona, hurting so bad.

Give up and get help, people said.
Pride blocks the way...I'll do it myself.
You'll never quit, the liar sneers, because you can't.

"Dear God! Can you help? I don't want to die."

You can't win the battle, but Jesus can.
He will break the padlock on your pit of affliction,
and carry you into the light.
Believe that He loves you and died on the cross,
to give you new life.
Take His hand, hold on tight.
Everything is possible for the one who believes.

"Dear God, my life is sinking sand.
You, O Lord, are solid rock.
Place your truth before my eyes and with it set me free from
agony and lies."

Paid in Full

The great news is that we have a forgiving God who loved us so much He gave His one and only Son for us, that whoever believes in Him will not perish, but instead will live forever (John 3:16). Jesus paid the consequences of my sin and yours. All you have to do is believe He did it for you, personally.

To talk to God about believing, you can pray your own prayer by just telling Him you want to believe in Jesus, you need your sins to be forgiven, and that to the best of your ability you are placing your life in His hands. Then, tell Him, "Thank you!"

CHAPTER 6

Finding Joy

Once I heard a pastor say that women need girlfriends. I think that's a good thing for husbands to know. It's not that we have a better time or more fun with our girlfriends, it's that we have a different kind of fun. Sometimes it's like therapy because women have feelings and emotions that men don't share. God made us that way—and He made men differently for a reason. Together, Charlie and I enjoy each other's company with the warmth and comfort of people who are happy in their marriages. Charlie has golfing buddies, and I enjoy time with girlfriends who have interests similar to mine.

In this chapter, you'll meet my best friend, Kathy. She didn't know how much she mattered to God!

Friends Forever

Kathy and I met over 40 years ago at a luncheon given for her because she had just moved into our area. I knew instantly that I liked Kathy because she had style! She was always so much fun, and totally real. She lived in the most impressive house I'd ever seen, yet she was so down-to-earth that she made everyone feel comfortable immediately.

In the early years of our friendship, we did things together with our children. We each had two little boys. Or, we went shopping and enjoyed drinking wine over lunch. In fact, there were four of us who were very close friends and we went on overnight shopping trips to Chicago twice a year. Our children were all in school by that time and we counted on our husbands to handle the home front for two days.

Kathy and I shared a hotel room during these trips. After a long day of shopping and dinner, the two of us ordered wine from room service and stayed up late drinking and gabbing. In the morning, we would finish any leftover wine, and then chew gum so the other girls wouldn't smell alcohol on our breath!

As time went on, our priorities got way out of whack. Drinking alcohol was the most important thing in our lives. We became alcoholics together.

Kathy knew she needed help because her husband told her she did. I wouldn't admit that I needed help. Charlie traveled a lot for work, so somehow, he didn't notice that I was in trouble. Occasionally, Kathy would suggest we go to AA together, but I always had a reason why I couldn't go— the unspoken reason being, "I don't want to."

Meanwhile, I was miserable. I had come to the point where I hated drinking as much as I loved it, and the hate was frightening because I knew I couldn't quit. You'll remember I was on a two-week trip to Hawaii with Charlie, when my drinking got so far out of control that I was afraid I might not survive the return flight. I ordered several little bottles of wine the first time the stewardess came by, and somehow my fragile self-made it home. It was then that God put the idea in my head to stop drinking for one day at a time and gave me the willpower to do it—even though I didn't know it was God.

After a week of not drinking, I told Kathy what was happening. She said, "Well! Then we're going to AA! I know where all the meetings are, and I'll pick you up at 11:30 tomorrow morning."

I thought, "Yikes! I don't want to go to AA—I'm only taking a break—I'm not quitting!" I figured if I had a break, maybe I could be a normal social drinker.

That cold snowy December day, I got into Kathy's car but when we got to the meeting I wouldn't go in! I lied and said that I would quit drinking with her—I just didn't want to go to meetings. She was miffed as she turned off the car's engine and left me sitting in the cold parking lot for an hour while she attended the meeting.

She came back and was very excited. She told me she was "going to do this thing and go to meetings every day for 30 days!" We agreed we would not drink and would call and be accountable to each other every day. She meant it...and she did it! I did it, too, but secretly I'd planned to start drinking again in January.

God, however, had other plans.

My big event of meeting Jesus was soon to take place! You'll remember from my testimony in Wit's End, that I had finally asked God for help. I was then invited to attend a Bible study. When I walked into the church where the Bible study was held, I was nervous. Oh, I hate to admit this now—I was dressed to impress all of the 'prim and proper' church ladies! And you'll laugh—they were lovely, friendly girls, some of whom I noticed carried expensive designer handbags! Over the years many became dear friends.

The biggest surprise was that the Bible itself turned out to be fascinating! Later, at home while doing my homework,

God used one verse, Matthew 13:22 to show me that my sin was choking Him out of my life. Suddenly, I knew it was true. He wiped the slate of my life clean and I knew that I belonged to Him for eternity! What a relief! Jesus rescued me and put me on the right path.

I was very excited about the changes God made in my life. No more denial, no delusions, no lying, and no fear. Instead, I was given a feeling of security, of joy, of hope, and the promise of a good future.

God also removed alcohol from my life. I thought I was taking a break. I didn't know it was a permanent break. I had planned to start drinking again sometime in January and tell Kathy that I wasn't really an alcoholic after all. But with God and Bible study on my mind, I postponed drinking again until June. It was an easy decision to make.

 I'll never forget the day it dawned on me that God had an altogether different idea. I was driving down the road, talking to God, when suddenly I said, "It was You who stopped my drinking! I knew it wasn't me!"

God said, "Yes."

I said, "And, I'm never going to drink again, am I?"

God said, "No."

A massive weight was lifted from my shoulders! And that thin, tan, rich woman with her crystal wine glasses, fancy clothes, and endless make-up, moved out of my mind for good! I was free! Wow, I belonged to God now, and that old life was gone!

With my whole new appreciation of the power of God, I wanted to tell other people about Jesus, the Savior. It was almost impossible, though, because most people didn't want to hear! So, I began praying to find a Christian friend, someone to share my excitement with.

I invited a lot of people to Bible study, especially Kathy, even though I had a hard time picturing her going because she smoked cigarettes, and, she often included a few curse words in her conversation. But, one day she shocked me and said she'd go!

Right away, God showed her, just like He did me, that every page of the Bible is full of truth and wisdom. She believed Him and turned her life over to Jesus. God answered my prayer for a Christian friend by turning Kathy, who was already my best friend, into a Christian. God is awesome!

The beauty of our story is that God did everything Himself. He did what we couldn't do for ourselves, and what no one else could do for us. He picked us up when we were drowning in alcohol, forgave our prideful and stubborn selfishness, and gave us love and a purpose. And a clean bill of health.

Kathy and I will be friends for eternity! And Jesus gets all the credit!

"Jesus said, 'I tell you the truth,
whoever hears my word and believes him who sent me
has eternal life and will not be condemned;
he has crossed over from death to life.'"
John 5:24

Kathy

My dear friend, Kathy, has graciously given me permission to share her story. She is an artist in Scottsdale, Arizona, and attends Scottsdale Bible Church. In her own words, this is how she met Jesus:

"I did not become a Christian until I was 50 years old. Then, when I did, I wondered why God waited so long. Now,

I am just thankful I belong to God. I did believe in God at that time; I just was not sure what Jesus had to do with the whole picture. I had not attended church or picked up a Bible for 30 years—30 years! —God forgive me."

"Four years before I became a Christian, I had awareness that I was an alcoholic. One morning, I awoke with a hangover so severe all I could do was lay on the floor in the bathroom. My boys, then 14 and 17, were quite used to this and paid little attention; they just went off to school. My wonderful husband, who was disappointed with me but continued to love me, shook his head and left for work."

"I called out to God. I begged God to help me because I couldn't help myself. Well, within days I was going to Alcoholics Anonymous (AA). Through AA's program, I realized it was God who was keeping me sober. The people at AA said that I could choose anything (such as a light bulb) as a Higher Power. I couldn't think of a light bulb as being of much help—so I leaned on God and let God be my Higher Power. The date I stopped drinking was December 2, 1988. Thank you, God! And thanks to God, I have not had a drink since then."

"As I continued to stay away from alcohol, my life started to come back together. My husband was a little wary of me, but my boys were great. One day I asked my younger son what he thought about my drinking—and I asked him what he hated the most when I was drinking. I thought he would say I embarrassed him or made a fool of myself, or something like that. But what he said still draws tears to my eyes just to think about it."

"He said, 'I was afraid I would come home from school and you would be dead.'"

"Talk about how our sins affect others. Can you believe it? The worst thing is, while I was drinking, I had such a low opinion of myself I thought my boys would be better off without me. I actually thought about ending my life. What a selfish person I was. Well, I still am selfish, but God is working on that!"

"During this time, I had a best friend. Her name was Betty, and she also had a problem with alcohol. She and I drank together, and then we were quitting together. I went to AA; she went to Bible study. After a few weeks in Bible study, she became a 'born-again Christian,' and I became sober. We talked every day. We were support for each other."

"She asked me to go to Bible study with her—for four years she asked me to go with her. At this time, God kept nudging me. I still had this empty hole in my heart, but my friend Betty seemed to glow. It was as if her hopelessness, emptiness, selfishness, and despair were gone. I wanted this! I wanted to know God like she did. I called her one day and said, 'OK, I'll go to Bible study.' She was shocked but made the arrangements. I began Bible study, praise God! It changed my whole life."

"The funny thing was, this Bible study was quite intense. Most of the girls were Christians. I had no clue how to read the Bible. I could have asked Betty but was too embarrassed. I did ask enough to get by—I mean, how do you tell someone you can't read the Bible? I had no idea what all the little numbers by the sentences were. I wasn't even sure what the books of the Bible were. So, I marched into class, got into my group, and told the leader I thought that since it was a Bible study, they should explain what all the little numbers were for. I can laugh now at why everyone was so helpful; they must have thought, 'Poor thing, she needs God.' I did need God, and I still need God."

"This was the last week of August, and on November 2, 1992, I put my soul into Jesus' hands. Thank you, God!"

"I remember that day. I was sitting at my dining room table, doing the homework for Bible study. A thought just popped into my head: 'This is true. This is real. I need to place my soul into Jesus' hands.' So, I thought, 'OK, I'm going to lay it all out and ask God to forgive me. But it will be a secret between God and me; I can't tell anyone.' I thought I wouldn't be able to face people—my gosh, me a born-again Christian—no one would believe it anyway. When I began to pray and weep over my awful sins, it was like lightning hit. I mean, I had this overwhelming feeling of peace, of joy, of wonder. I know now what I felt was the presence of God."

"Well, I thought, 'Now, I have to tell everyone!' I kept thinking that since I didn't know any of this, all of my unbelieving friends must not know either. 'I have to tell them. I have to let them in on this joy,' I thought."

"Well, I don't need to tell you—they did not want to hear this. You see, I only had one Christian friend; all of my other friends were non-Christians, or as I heard a pastor once say, 'Pre-Christians.' I remember my husband used to say as we were getting ready to go out with a group, 'Please, Kathy, don't bring up Jesus.' Poor man—I couldn't help myself!"

"Oh, how my life has changed. Jesus just took over. I hardly know what all to tell. I will say that it has not all been great because life is a series of ups and downs. But even the bad today is better than my best used to be without God. I know now that I can 'do all things through Christ, who gives me strength' Philippians 4:13

"Thank goodness God only changes you a bit at a time—my gosh, if He were to have changed me all at once, I would have died of shock and so would my family. God began small. First, He removed my foul language. Would you believe I thought it was very smart to use gutter words? What a fool I was."

"Also, at this time I smoked cigarettes. I noticed that no one at Bible study smoked. I thought maybe I wasn't representing God very well by smoking, so I talked to God about it. I told God that I loved to smoke and didn't really want to quit, but if He wanted me to, I would. I just could not do this on my own, I told Him; He would have to do it for me."

"Months went by—then, bang, God was ready! I got up one morning and was so distracted I forgot to smoke. Now—if you are a smoker or an ex-smoker, you know that you do not forget to smoke! Noon arrived on the clock and I thought, 'Oh no, God! This is the day I'm going to quit smoking, isn't it?' It was! Oh, our gracious God, He took this, too, away from me—just took it, poof! God is great!"

"My years with God have been the most wonderful years I ever had. I don't know how to live without God anymore—I don't know how other people can. I don't know how I made it 50 years—50 wasted years—the emptiness, selfishness, hopelessness, fleeting pleasure, the total feeling of doom. I do know this: I now have a desire to know God more, to love others, and to do the best I can in all situations. And I don't have to do this alone. I have God! Thank you, Jesus!"

"So, in closing, I will say, 'All is well, all is well with my soul!' My prayer is that each day, whether I get anything else done, I pray I will spend time loving God and loving other people, because that's what life is all about—and I don't want to waste a day!"

"'...and all the angels shouted for joy.'"
Job 38:7

*"The Lord has done great things for us,
and we are filled with joy."*
Psalm 126:3

Choose Joy

You can hear the joy in Kathy's voice, right? God's Holy Spirit has poured that joy into her life. Each person who believes in Jesus receives the gift of the Holy Spirit, who comes to live in his or her heart. That's how close our heavenly Father is to us!

When you are a Christian, joy is a profound and permanent treasure. It's there even when bad news arrives and when hearts are heavy. No one can steal your joy because nothing can separate you from God's grip. You may have to choose to be grateful and joyful when life's challenges undermine your joy, but you can do that! You can make a decision to smile when you rehearse the truth that God is for you, and you are His forever.

For me, joy is a deep-seated feeling of security that I belong to Jesus, and no matter what happens, I'm His and I'm OK! (And, yes, sometimes I still have to choose joy on days when other thoughts erase it all.)

"Shout with joy to God, all the earth!
Say to God, 'How awesome are your deeds!'"
Psalm 66:1-3

"Because your love is better than life,
I will praise you as long as I live."
Psalm 63:3-4

"This is the day the Lord has made;
let us be glad and rejoice in it."
Psalm 118:24

CHAPTER 7

Jesus is the Answer

Are you wondering if it really matters if you believe in God and accept His Son Jesus as your savior? To be honest, for 46 years I hoped the part about Jesus didn't really matter. Why in the world was the name Jesus so unnerving to me? I mean, God had to practically hit me over the head and drag me into His Kingdom! I can't put my finger on the reason, except to say I thought I'd be missing out on what the world had to offer. And to me, the name Jesus meant having to submit to someone I didn't want to submit to. Now when I compare what the world had to offer with what life with Jesus is like, there's no comparison. It was ordinary versus wondrous, drudgery versus thrilling.

Whew! I'm so glad I didn't miss out! A big thank you to Jesus! And I'm not forced to submit to Him—I want to do things His way because the results are miraculous.

Once I saw what life with Jesus was like, I wanted everyone to believe. When I told friends, some of the responses were, "That's fine for you, but I don't need God," or "I believe in

God, just not the 'Jesus' part." This chapter shines light on the answers to those responses.

For those who don't know, I wish I could add a flashing neon sign right here that says, "You matter to God and He loves you!"

Banking on God

Sometimes people find it hard to believe in God because of the "why" question. Why does God let bad things happen? You can see when bad things happen as a direct consequence of your own actions—I surely can. But, more often than not you can't see any immediate reason for the difficulties you face. There is, however, a way you can still believe in God and trust Him.

I went to Bible study wondering if there really is a place called hell, and why bad things happen. I found out right away that hell is real (Matthew 13:30, 40-47, Matthew 10:28). Also, trials are a "given" (1 Thessalonians 3:2-3).

But all of that bad news was completely countered by meeting Jesus and putting my life in His hands. Seeing for the very first time that Jesus is God, and every word of the Bible is true, totally enveloped my mind. Any questions I still had were forgotten by the overwhelming reality and majesty of God Himself. I belonged to God now and that was all that mattered anymore!

The joy of knowing the truth and knowing He loves me was and is all I need. As I watched Him make a profound difference in my life and the lives of others, God unquestionably became my strength, my confidence, and my awesome answer to everything in life. I know He has my back no matter what happens.

And the funny thing is, I saw the truth right away—one month into Bible study. That's because faith comes through hearing and reading the good news about Jesus Christ

(Romans 10:17). Following that, when you turn to the Lord, the veil that covers your heart is taken away. Jesus opens your mind and heart so you can understand the scriptures (2 Corinthians 3:15-16; Luke 24:45).

All you and I need for the rest of our lives is to belong to Jesus and understand the Bible He wrote. Now we have crossed the only hurdle for having faith when everything seems to contradict God, because we can trust who God is—His flawless character.

Yes, I'm caught off guard from time to time, but from here on in, when trouble strikes, I will turn to God first (not last) and make it my "job" to counteract worry and Satan's lies with the truth that God knows, cares, and loves me. He is with me moment-by-moment and will never leave. He does have a plan and will not forsake me. Whew, a touch of peace sets in and begins to grow right away.

> *"Do not let your hearts be troubled.*
> *Trust in God, trust also in me."*
> (Jesus speaking in John 14:1)

> *"I have told you these things,*
> *so that in me you may have peace.*
> *In this world you will have trouble. But take heart!*
> *I have overcome the world."*
> John 16:33

He Cannot Lie

A powerful, magnificent, and unchangeable fact is that God cannot lie. People can lie, but God cannot. It's impossible for Him to lie because He is holy and perfect. There is no darkness in Him. He is light, He is truth, He is pure. Since God—who is God the Father, God the Son, and God the Holy Spirit—cannot lie, it means His promises to us are rock solid and unbreakable. You and I can bank our lives on them (Hebrews 6:18; Titus 1:2).

Because God is holy and pure, He is always good. It is unthinkable that He would do wrong. He is a faithful God and you can count on Him to do everything well (Job 34:12, Deuteronomy 32:4, Mark 7:37).

There's more! His wisdom is profound. He is perfect in knowledge. The riches and depth of His wisdom, knowledge, and judgments are unsearchable; His paths are beyond tracing out (Job 9:4, Job 37:16, Romans 11:33).

Can you see why my confidence in God soared when His attributes became a reality for me, and, when He proved Himself through His Word and through what He did for me and my family? The fact that God cannot lie fascinates me. When I let that sink in, it becomes a marvelous blanket of assurance around me. It guarantees that God—who is gracious, loving, merciful, and forgiving—will never leave me, and will work all things together ultimately for my good and always for His Glory because He loves me, and I love Him.

"For if, when we were God's enemies,
we were reconciled to him through the death of his Son,
how much more, having been reconciled,
shall we be saved through his life!"
Romans 5:10

"And we know that in all things God works
for the good of those who love him,
who have been called according to his purpose."
Romans 8:28

On the Fence?

Are you on the fence about having a one-on-one relationship with Jesus? Maybe your life is fine right now—no negatives. The thing is, at some point in everyone's life, something bad happens. It just does. Serious illness, loss of a job, divorce, or any other challenge can suddenly throw you into a tailspin. Many times, this will be the impetus that brings a person to Jesus, and that's a wonderful thing, because whether or not your life turns out the way you hoped it would, belonging to Jesus is the most comforting place to be. He has so many ways to help you through the tough times. Missing out on God's resources even for everyday life would be costly.

But there's an even more important reason than having help when life turns upside down, and that is something everyone has to face sooner or later—what happens when you die?

The Bible says God created you, loves you, and wants a never-ending relationship with you. He makes this possible for those who trust Jesus instead of themselves. The Gospel is easy to understand—sin separates you from God. And the only way to bridge the gap between yourself and God is to believe in Jesus, who died on the cross in your place to take the consequences for your sin. Once you believe, you become "right with God," and it's a huge relief.

It means your sins are forgiven and you'll be going to heaven. That's a gift you can't get by any other means.

Everyone has an incredible choice to make in life. You can listen to the voice of human reason or to God's voice. In times of trouble, self-help motivators and human philosophy may produce a temporary fix, but neither will work long term and they will cause you to forfeit the blessings that could have been yours with God leading the way. Whether tragedy strikes or life is "smooth sailing," God offers wisdom, guidance, forgiveness, joy, and peace of mind. More than that, He gives purpose and meaning to your life.

"'Here I am!
I stand at the door and knock.
If anyone hears my voice and opens the door,
I will come in and eat with him, and he with me.'"
Jesus speaking in Revelation 3:20

"This is what the Lord says:
'Stand at the crossroads and look;
ask for the ancient paths,
ask where the good way is and walk in it,
and you will find rest for your souls.'"
Jeremiah 6:16

"'Whether you turn to the right or to the left,
your ears will hear a voice behind you, saying,
'This is the way; walk in it.'"
Isaiah 30:21

How Do You See God?

When I was growing up, my view of God was that He was a distant God who created everything and took care of it all. I thought He had much better things to do than to worry about anything I might be praying about. Consequently, if I prayed at all, my prayers were repetitious and boring.

I was quite delighted when I learned at Bible study that I should be praying specifically for small things and big things. My group leader suggested I write down my prayers and watch for God's answers so I could thank Him. I began praying very specific and personal prayers for myself, my husband, and our boys. It was exciting to see answers. Often, a long time passed before I saw an answer, but when I did, it was a gift from God that I never forgot. An example would be when God told me to love Charlie unconditionally and I asked Him to please make me love Charlie. It took time, but the Lord's answer is on display every day now in our marriage.

When Jesus took over my thinking, my view of God changed dramatically as I began to see Him as my Father in heaven. Fortunately, my own father was an incredible example of a father's love. So, when I discovered how much God loved me, it was easy for me to picture what that love looked like. It looked like the love a parent has for a child! And it feels like a genuine hug—all the time!

Whether your view of God is similar, skewed, or vague, my heart's desire is for you to know how very much God loves you, and for you to know His Son, Jesus, who loves you so much He was willing to die for you. He wants you to grasp how wide and long and high and deep His love is (Ephesians 3:18-19). He wants you to be immersed in His soothing, reassuring, and permanent love. He calls you His "Beloved."

"'Let the beloved of the Lord rest secure in him,
for he shields him all day long,
and the one the Lord loves rests between his shoulders.'"
Deuteronomy 33:12

"How great is the love the Father has lavished on us,
that we should be called children of God!
And that is what we are!"
1 John 3:1

You Matter to God

You are the Lord's beloved. You are irreplaceable. You were not created aimlessly or insignificantly. You were purposefully and marvelously made by the Creator of the Universe, who makes no mistakes. He formed your inward parts and provided for you in your mother's womb. You are precious in His sight and treasured in His heart.

He is acquainted with all your ways. He perceives your thoughts from afar. Before a word is on your tongue, He knows it completely. God is interested in every facet of your life, because He designed you with a purpose. Before you were born, plans were in place for you to bring a unique and special glory to His Name, through Jesus Christ.

It doesn't matter how much your parents did or didn't contribute to your well-being, God has a plan for your life! It doesn't matter what your gifts are or aren't, or what disadvantages you face, God has a plan for you. Are you curious? It's never too late to find out!

Your Father in heaven knows you and loves you more than anybody else. His love will surround you, comfort you, and build you up when you are down. His love is always kind, always protects, and will never let go of you. His love never fails.

You were created to know God, to love Him, and be loved by Him forever. He himself set eternity in your heart. Don't miss it, beloved! Take Jesus to be your Lord and your Savior, your day planner, your guardian and your answer to everything.

"Though the mountains be shaken
and the hills be removed,
yet my unfailing love for you will not be shaken..."
Isaiah 54:10

For further reference: Psalm139:3-4,13, Genesis 1:27, Deuteronomy 32:4, Psalm 72:12-13, Psalm 33:15, Psalm 138:8, Ephesians 2:10, Jeremiah 31:3, 1 John 3:1, 1 Corinthians 13:4-5, Ecclesiastes 3:11, John 3:16

CHAPTER 8

God's Love: Up Close and Personal

Did you know that God's goals for Christians are to love Him first, to love others, to tell them about Jesus, and to bring glory to God's name? I think bringing glory to God means doing things that bring honor and attention to God—things that show others how awesome He really is. It means doing loving, kind things that go above and beyond what anyone expects so that God gets the credit when others notice. We do it because we love God, and He loves the person we're serving.

In this chapter you'll get a glimpse up close and personal of what it's like to lovingly serve a child with special needs because God loves that child. The child is our grandson, Turner. He is Matt and Rebecca's son.

God's Impeccable Timing

When I was the only one in the household who knew Jesus personally, I used to think about who would be the next one to believe. I decided it would be Matt, the youngest, because Steve and Charlie, were both Type A personalities who thought they pretty much knew everything. How in the world was God ever going to get them to believe? Matt, on the other hand, was such a nice kid I figured if I told him about Jesus he would say, "That sounds good, Mom, how do I do this?" He was always easy going, tender hearted, and fiercely loyal to his family and friends.

The fact that Steve was first was inconceivable. I wasn't even sure it was true when he called home from law school at the University of Iowa and told me. He said, "Mom, you were right. Now I know Jesus is God. I don't know how I know—but I know." I was so excited, yet I wondered if it was real. Then he came home for the weekend, and I actually saw a change in him. For one thing, he wanted to go to church with me. The beauty of God's timing in reaching Steve first was that his father and brother couldn't miss seeing the difference in him.

Matt was in college, and whenever he was home for a weekend or for the summer, I would ask him to go to church. Occasionally he would go. God's pursuit of him was similar to His pursuit of Steve, and Matt's reaction was much the same. He would seem interested, then again, he wasn't.

The pastor at Gracespring Bible Church at that time, Larry Kiser, was a very gifted Bible teacher. Honestly, my mind would never wander when he was preaching. One Sunday, it was just Matt and me at church and I thought he'd heard the best possible message for where he was in his journey to Jesus. When we got in the car afterwards, my typically calm, easy-going kid pounded on the steering wheel and said, "I didn't agree with a thing pastor Larry said!"

I was shocked but kept still. On the way home he stopped at a coffee shop, and while he was in getting coffee, I prayed and asked God for just one sentence I could say to Matt that would give him some insight. While I did receive an answer, how I wish I had written that sentence down because I don't remember it now. It was perfect for changing Matt's whole demeanor. What I do remember is that the sentence started with, "Matt, have you ever thought about...?"

One thing I knew for sure—he was in church that morning for a reason. He just didn't know it yet.

Another time, when Matt was home for the weekend and hadn't gone to church in quite a while, I got him to agree that he wouldn't stay out too late on Saturday night and would go to church in the morning. He stayed out way too late, but I woke him up the next morning anyway and he honored his agreement.

Before the message, pastor Larry told the audience to open their Bibles to a certain chapter—or open the pew Bible to a certain page number—then stand and read aloud together. I couldn't believe my eyes when Matt took the pew Bible, opened it, and read the designated verses. This was a big, big deal. I was so thrilled I was afraid I might tear up, and if he saw me get emotional over it, I was sure he would close the Bible and put it back. So, I quickly prayed, "Dear God, thank you, and please don't let me cry!" I didn't cry, and Matt continued to read aloud those precious Words from God.

A friend of mine who was sitting behind us in church told me later she had been praying for Matt from the time she saw him walk in with Charlie and me. It warms my heart to know God hears and answers prayers.

The rather comical part of this very serious work of God is that later, after Matt was a believer in Jesus, he went to church with us one Sunday and afterwards smiled and said, "That was great. I needed a good dose of pastor Larry!" God is so faithful!

"Jesus answered,
'Man does not live on bread alone,
but on every word that comes from the mouth of God.'"
Matthew 4:4

"Your word is a lamp to my feet
and a light for my path."
Psalm 119:105

"I will never forget your precepts, for by them you have preserved my life. Save me, for I am yours."

The Life Changing Power of Christ

Matt is now senior director of ticket marketing at the PGA Tour global headquarters in Ponte Vedra Beach, Florida. He and his wife Rebecca and their two children attend The Church of Eleven 22 (non-denominational) in Jacksonville. In Matt's own words, he writes of how he came to know Jesus, and also what it is like for him to be the father of a child with special needs.

"When I was in college, I believed in God, but my religion was my own version—and it was loosely based on three things: God exists, He ultimately wants good things for me, and, all things are held together in the universe by Him. The problem with that version of faith was it was self-serving, and it wasn't personal. It's not the kind of faith that carries a person through tough times. Thankfully, Jesus is always pursuing people and He didn't give up on me."

"Life is full of different seasons—some are short and marked by big changes; other seasons can last a long time. I met Jesus during a season of major change taking place in my life. After college graduation, I was trying to figure out what to do with my life, while dealing with a long-distance relationship."

"It was fortunate that God led me to Houston where I spent time living with my brother and his wife, Jody. They were both Christians, going to church regularly, and hanging out with other Christians. I knew my brother had been 'saved' but I didn't really come to understand what that meant until I lived with him for those four months. There were noticeable changes in his lifestyle; his behavior was different, his attitude was different and the source of his joy and peace was coming from his faith, not from his circumstances."

"During that time, I was great at faking that everything was OK, but I felt pretty lost on the inside. I didn't have a good plan on where to go next or what to do with my life anymore. I prayed often that God would help me figure it out. I had a lot of conversations with Steve about Jesus and what 'being saved' was all about. I never felt much like a sinner, but that was really me just lying to myself. Jesus didn't give up on me and there were several nights where I prayed to Jesus to come into my life and take over. I was done trying to live life on my own. I was going to trust in Jesus as my Savior and do life His way."

"A few days later, I prayed that prayer publicly with Steve and some of his friends during a run around Memorial Park. When you give your life over to Jesus—and you understand what following Jesus means, it changes how you think about everything—you don't have to experience this life alone—and there's a real peace about that, even in tough and uncertain times."

"This is often where testimonials end, but it's important to understand how Jesus continued to walk with me through another season in my life. A challenging season—and a season that may last the rest of my days on Earth. A season that, without Jesus being right next to me, would have shattered my own version of religion and broken me.

"Nothing magical happened after I was saved. There was some relief, like a weight was lifted from me. God took away some worry as I learned that I could trust in Him. I spent more time praying and reading the Bible, and without really knowing what was happening, God started to build up my courage and strength."

"With a strange peace about the unknown, I packed up a U-Haul and drove it into New York City, where Rebecca was living, to see if she really was 'the one' I believed she was. I prayed that God would help me find a place to live, and a job, and that if it was meant to be with Rebecca, that it would all work out."

"Well God answered those prayers! The one friend I knew from college who lived in New York helped me find a place to live, and a job in advertising. Two years later, Rebecca and I got married."

"You know what I never prayed much about? Finding a good church. Well, God's plan for me was at work and God knew exactly what I needed because after trying a dozen different churches in Manhattan, we started attending Tim Keller's Redeemer Presbyterian Church, and even though I didn't know it at the time—it was an essential gift from Jesus. Tim Keller is one of the most respected pastors in the world and he has written numerous best-selling books. Little did I know how God was going to speak to me through Keller."

"God blessed our family and answered many prayers throughout a big transition from New York to Chicago. In 2004, our daughter Chloe was born, and she immediately brought us amazing joy and brought us closer to God than we ever thought possible. In terms of how our culture measures success, I felt we were on track. Good jobs, healthy marriage, life in the big city."

"In 2006, our son Turner was born. He had special needs, and his arrival marked the start of a new season in my life. Our whole world was turned upside down. I spent a lot of time praying for miracles that didn't happen; asking God the 'why me' questions. I read every Bible story about Jesus healing someone; wrote them all down and studied them. The interesting thing is that in almost every instance of Jesus healing someone physically or emotionally, the person healed had been sick for a very long time."

"God's timeline is often different from the timeline you've prayed for—that was something Keller pointed out. Keller has written a lot about pain and suffering, and after wrestling with a lot of questions about why God allowed Turner to be born with special needs, Jesus spoke to me through Keller as I was taking Turner to school one morning in Florida. I was listening to an old sermon of Keller's and Jesus laid on my heart this question: 'What if God is actually using your pain and suffering to protect you from something much worse? Like not having a relationship with God at all?'"

"Our circumstances with Turner's special needs have taught me a lot about God over the years. But back to the Keller question—and maybe the most important thing I've learned is that God is using Turner's disability to keep my heart close to God's heart. Jesus is using my circumstances with Turner as a shield to protect me from a life apart from Him. Even though I know I'm saved by God's grace, I have no choice but to stay in a relationship with Jesus—pray regularly—ask Him for strength—help—just to get through the day. The Bible often points out how easy it is to drift apart from God. This is true for me. Especially in today's culture and in the place where we live. It's so easy to let the things of this world rule our hearts—even good things like career, family, children, money. How easy is it for us to get distracted by these things? To forget about Jesus? To get caught up in the material successes of this world? To act like we are the ones in control?"

"The Bible says in Mark 10:45: 'For even the Son of Man did not come to be served, but to serve, and to give His life as a ransom for many.' Our culture teaches us the opposite—how do I set up life so my needs are met? That's what our culture preaches. The problem with that is it's not how Jesus lived or wants me to live. By blessing me and my family with Turner, Jesus is showing us how much joy and peace we can have (even in difficult circumstances) by serving Turner's needs—seeing him laugh and smile—and knowing that one day in heaven, Jesus himself will wipe away every tear—and everything sad about Turner will become untrue. Just as He tells us in the book of Revelation:

"And I heard a loud voice from the throne saying, 'Now the dwelling of God is with men, and he will live with them. They will be his people, and God himself will be with them and be their God. He will wipe every tear from their eyes. There will be no more death or mourning or crying or pain, for the old order of things has passed away.' He who was seated on the throne said, 'I am making everything new!' Then he said, 'Write this down, for these words are trustworthy and true.'" (Revelation 21:3-5)

"Turner is full of the Holy Spirit—he softens even the hardest of hearts, including mine. Jesus didn't send Turner to 'save' me—only Jesus can save me—but now it's very clear to me that Jesus is using our circumstances to keep me close to Him and protect me. And Jesus is walking beside Turner and me with every step. Now I feel that death from this life isn't scary because one day, I'll have my family in heaven, and being with Jesus for eternity will be our reward."

How My Special Needs Son Taught Me Lessons in Christianity

"While Turner's walk with canes is challenging, filled with falls, bumps, and bruises, as his father, my love never waivers and I'm there to encourage him every step of the way. I marvel in his triumphs even though for most typical kids, Turner's success in life is not on the world's scale. Our Father in heaven's love for us is like that, too.

"Turner is nonverbal. That makes it hard to communicate as father and son. This makes me wonder what God is trying to tell me that I can't understand.

"Any person in this world can make a difference if they are filled with the Holy Spirit. Turner, at age 13, has done more to soften hearts than most do in a lifetime.

"Patience, oh the patience a father has with his son, whom he loves dearly. How much patience has God had with me?

"When I'm away from our home, I miss Turner. God wants to be with us every day.

"Turner loves DVDs—not watching them, just holding them, reading the words printed on them and spinning them around his thumb. I know that he likes certain ones best. I buy the ones I think he will enjoy the most. I read the words on them that he points to because he likes to hear the words out loud. Jesus knows what every one of us likes, just as I know Turner likes DVDs. I like golf more than most, even avid golfers, and was fortunate to play Cypress Point and Pebble Beach. That reminded me that God knows me and gives me gifts specifically designed for me.

"I saw Tim Tebow at church the other day. It reminded me of how God looks at me, Turner, and Tebow—we're all the same in His eyes—sons of the Most High King.

"God's plans are greater than my plans. He loves Turner more than I can fathom which is hard to grasp. He knows the plans He has for Turner. I will trust that.

"Turner changed my perspective on heaven. It always seemed like a safe place people go to be with Jesus. True. Now I'm looking forward to doing father and son things in heaven with Turner.

"Turner might be a great warrior in heaven. He might be a scratch golfer, too."

Leaning on God

With the marvelous addition of Matt's faith in Jesus, a verse from the Bible finally came true for our family. It was 10 years from the time Jesus rescued me until all four of us believed.

"...choose for yourselves this day whom you will serve...
as for me and my household, we will serve the Lord."
Joshua 24:15

When Turner was born, we realized what a lifeline our faith was to us. We knew a couple who had an adult special needs son in a wheelchair, and their experiences gave us a picture of what Turner's future life could look like—but we hoped for something better for him. I thank God that we had enough faith to know that whatever would lie ahead, God knew about it, and we wouldn't have to face it alone. Nevertheless, from what the doctors were saying, Turner's future looked bleak, and we prayed as never before.

I know now that God was working behind the scenes the whole time, but I didn't think about it then. I also know that Matt and Rebecca chose to trust God and accept a challenge that costs them in many ways yet brings glory to God daily as they care for their son. They are doing as much as possible to give him and his sister every opportunity to blossom and pursue God's plan for their lives. It isn't easy, but God makes a way even when there seems to be no way, and, He provides many unexpected blessings.

When Turner was born, he was in the hospital neonatal unit for over two months. He came home with a feeding tube that dripped nutrition slowly, around the clock, and needed to be changed every few hours. He couldn't swallow or self-soothe, and there seemed to be no way to comfort him. If he was awake, he was crying—and he woke up a lot.

Rebecca eventually got him to take a pacifier, but it wouldn't stay in his mouth. This meant if he was awake, we needed to hold him to make sure the pacifier stayed in place so his crying wouldn't get out of hand and cause a seizure. Rebecca found something at Walgreen's that we called "dip juice" for the pacifier. It was just a harmless flavored liquid that we dipped the pacifier into so Turner would take it again if it fell out of his mouth. It was a life saver.

Every two weeks, Rebecca's parents and I took turns going to Chicago to help. Sleep was at a premium. Many times I sat in a chair in the master bedroom in the wee hours of the morning, next to the IV pole, holding Turner and the "dip juice" for the pacifier, hoping to keep him comfortable and quiet so his parents could sleep in the same room until it was time to get up, or until Chloe woke up. I loved holding Turner and I prayed the whole time. I prayed I wouldn't doze off and let my finger slip off the pacifier which would cause Turner to cry!

Those were difficult days. I cried often and leaned on God. I survived by the grace of God and His strength. I knew it was His strength because I sure didn't have any of my own.

We all survived on the best macaroni and cheese ever, made by one of the cooks at Children's Hospital! Turner was in and out of that hospital, and every time we were there, we brought containers of macaroni and cheese home with us—an extra blessing from God!

"Look to the Lord and his strength;
seek his face always."
Psalm 105:4

Superstars

It's comforting to know that Turner is God's precious boy. God created him, and He loves him. He sees Turner as having special abilities! And, like the blind man in the Bible, God chose Turner to bring a unique and wonderful Glory to God's name.

"'Before I formed you in the womb,
I knew you, before you were born, I set you apart...'"
Jeremiah 1:5

"Jesus' disciples asked Him about a blind man,
saying, 'Rabbi, who sinned, this man or his parents,
that he was born blind?'
Jesus said, 'Neither this man nor his parents sinned,
but this happened so that the works of God
might be displayed in him.'"
John 9:2-3

And that is happening with Turner! Through Turner and his family, people can see God's love up close, and God gets the glory. God designed life, love, and families. He knows the tender hearts of this family as they walk a difficult path, and He walks with them as they face the trials few other families have to face. God is right there, surprising them with laughter, joy, and blessings along the way. He appointed them to His service, and He considers them faithful. In fact, He sees them as superstars!

"I thank Christ Jesus our Lord,
who has given me strength,
that he considers me trustworthy,
appointing me to his service."
1 Timothy 1:12

"An argument started among the disciples
as to which of them would be the greatest.
Jesus, knowing their thoughts,
took a little child and had him stand beside him.
Then he said to them,
'Whoever welcomes this little child in my name,
welcomes me; and whoever welcomes me
welcomes the one who sent me.
For he who is least among you all—he is the greatest.'"
Luke 9:46-48

"And God is able to bless you abundantly,
so that in all things at all times,
having all that you need,
you will abound in every good work."
2 Corinthians 9:8

When You Don't Get Your Miracle

When Turner was four, the pastor of Matt and Rebecca's church, Joby Martin, saw them park in a handicap space, pile out of the car, and get the wheelchair out for Turner. He watched Turner's sister, Chloe, just 18 months older, push Turner into the Sunday School area. Later, he met with them and asked if he could make a short DVD of their family to illustrate one of his messages about trusting God daily in a difficult situation.

It was a sweet video that the pastor showed the congregation, and then talked about what to do when the storm you are in seems bigger than life. He titled his message, "Where is Your Faith?" and asked the question, "What do you do when you pray for a miracle and the Miracle Maker doesn't come through for you?" He outlined three important points. I watched his message several times online and wrote them down as accurately as I could. Pastor Joby gave me permission to share from my notes as follows:

"Put your faith in Jesus Christ, no matter what. Your life can either be driven by fear of your circumstances, or by faith in the one who is Lord over your circumstances. If Jesus says, 'Let's go over to the other side of the lake,' it means you'll be going to the other side, even if there's a storm on the way. And when Jesus said that to His disciples in Luke 8:22, He fell asleep as they sailed. What does that tell us? He was not worried; He had everything under control."

"Pray the words of Habakkuk 3:19. Sovereign Lord, you are my strength. Make my feet like the feet of a deer, Lord. Since you've marked out the race for me, give me the feet to run the race that you have called me to run. Because if you will do that, then you'll enable me to go on to the heights. You'll discipline me to maturity, and you will use the storms of my life to take me to places I would never have gone on my own. If I had to choose it—I don't think I would choose this path. But since you are Sovereign and you chose that path for me, let me walk it in a way that I cannot do alone. I need your power, Lord, to make my feet like the feet of a deer so that you can take me to the heights."

"Grab on to Daniel 3:17-18. This is the account of Shadrach, Meshach, and Abednego. It was a case of 'bow down to the idol,' or capital punishment. It's a choice they had to make and one that we must make—fear or faith—

you choose. The Gospel is not 'serve God because He will fix you up.' You must put your faith in Jesus Christ no matter what. Jesus says, 'Follow Me.' That is the Gospel. And on this Earth, following Him may increase the storms of life. The difference is that God has every detail of your storm and your life under control. He has a plan and a purpose. Shadrach, Meshach, and Abednego said to the king, 'The God we serve is able to save us—He will rescue us from your hand—but even if He does not—we will not serve your gods.'"

"We must believe that God is able to show up in a miraculous way. We must praise Him. And, we must say, 'I believe that He will calm the storm, but even if He doesn't, I'm choosing to trust Him!'"[4]

Joby Martin is the lead pastor at The Church of Eleven 22 in Jacksonville, FL, and a national speaker. I'm thankful he allowed me to share these 3 truths that have encouraged me to get in the boat with Jesus during the storms of my life, trusting Him for the rescue. Charlie and I enjoy hearing Pastor Joby preach when we visit Matt and Rebecca. Joby 'tells it like it is,' presenting the truth of Jesus with great clarity. With Southern warmth, he holds your attention, making the marvelous Word of God personal. He can touch your heart and bring tears to your eyes. He will make you smile with his humor. Formerly a youth pastor, he appeals to all ages.

> *"One day Jesus said to his disciples,*
> *'Let's go over to the other side of the lake.'*
> *So, they got into a boat and set out.*
> *As they sailed, he fell asleep.*
> *A squall came down on the lake,*
> *so that the boat was being swamped,*
> *and they were in great danger.*
> *The disciples went and woke him, saying,*

'Master, Master, we're going to drown!'
He got up and rebuked the wind and the raging waters;
the storm subsided, and all was calm.
'Where is your faith?' he asked his disciples.
In fear and amazement, they asked one another,
'Who is this? He commands even the winds and the water,
and they obey him.'
Luke 8:22-25

God is at the Helm

As Turner's grandmother, I know that God's blessings of courage, patience, and strength are evident in Matt and Rebecca's lives.

Some people say God doesn't give us more than we can handle. Actually, that's not true. In the Bible, the apostle Paul writes that he and his companions suffered hardships and were under such great pressure—far beyond their ability to endure—that they even despaired of life. Paul goes on to say, "This happened that we might not rely on ourselves but on God, who raises the dead." (2 Corinthians 1:8-9)

This is something you can apply to your life. If you come to the point of knowing you're at a complete loss in managing your circumstances, your only hope is to trust God because if He can raise the dead—and He did—He will handle your situation. You can be sure of that.

It's easy to confuse temptations, for which God does provide a way out—with trials, for which God may choose to provide a way "through," instead (See 1 Corinthians 10:12-13 for temptations; 2 Corinthians 1:8-9 for trials).

From the bewildering unknowns and living in survival mode with very little sleep the first couple of years in Turner's life, along with hopes and milestones not reached, and prayers seemingly unanswered, God has given Matt and Rebecca

His guidance. Sometimes, His leadership was specific when they felt lost in their pressing challenges.

When God moved Matt and his family from Chicago to Florida, we thought it was for Matt's dream job in the world of golf. Rebecca was apprehensive about leaving Turner's therapists in Chicago. She then realized the move was as much for Turner as it was for Matt, since there were wonderful therapists for Turner in Florida and a marvelous school for special needs children.

Turner has prospered and learned so many things in Florida. He's a whiz with an iPad! He finds so much joy in his family and even though he doesn't talk, he'll belly laugh while playing with the garden hose as if it was a big water fountain. God's care and power are unmistakable in Turner's life.

"'For I know the plans I have for you,' declares the Lord,
'plans to prosper you and not to harm you,
plans to give you hope and a future.'"
Jeremiah 29:11

"'My grace is sufficient for you,
for my power is made perfect in weakness.'"
2 Corinthians 12:9

I Can Only Imagine

Does it seem unfair that some people live with lifelong struggles? With respect to Turner's experience, I've seen the challenges for Matt and Rebecca in raising a special needs child, for Turner being the special needs child who wants to be like everybody else, and for Chloe, being a sister who has extra responsibilities. For others, I've seen parents in grief over losing a child, friends suffering from physical and emotional pain due to abuse, illness, injuries from war, fire, swimming, hunting, or car accidents, and more. There is a great amount of human suffering in this world. God's people are called to be the hands and feet of Jesus, lovingly serving others.

As a Christian, you want to do your absolute best to serve God here on Earth. You often wonder exactly how God wants you to do this. I've thought that perhaps people who are navigating extreme challenges never have to wonder how they are to serve God. I've come to believe they are daily serving Him by accepting the challenges, and to the best of their ability, showing others a glimpse of God's heart, His love and compassion, His strength, and His peace. Even by allowing a smile to break through their burdens, they display the splendor of God in contrast to difficult circumstances.

I also believe their reward in heaven will be breathtaking beyond imagination. All of the heartbreak they've known on Earth will become heart-pounding excitement when they see everything that was so wrong be made right and beautiful in heaven. No one else will have exactly that same indescribable reversal of events that a parent who has lost a child or cared for a loved one with devastating challenges will have. I can only imagine....

The Bible says there will be rewards in heaven conforming to your good works— according to how you have served God in the life He gave you. While you will only gain entrance to heaven if you believe in Jesus (and not because of your good works on Earth so that no one can boast), once you're there, you will be rewarded for what you have done to serve your Savior, Jesus Christ.

"Always give yourselves fully to the work of the Lord,
because you know that your labor
in the Lord is not in vain."
1 Corinthians 15:58

No eye has seen, no ear has heard,
no mind has conceived
what God has prepared for those who love him."
1 Corinthians 2:9

He Comforts Me

When dreams are dashed and you have a life that's not like most others because yours is very difficult, and it appears theirs is not—when you're disappointed and struggling with no end in sight—count on and rehearse what you know to be true:

God knows your name.

He knows how hard your days and nights are.

He loves you more than you can imagine.

And loves your family the same.

He will provide for you and will strengthen you.

He will bless you and protect you.

He has plans to prosper you in your current circumstances.

He will direct your path.

He will walk with you and will carry you.

He will give you rest and a peace that is beyond human understanding.

He will never leave you nor forsake you.

You can lean on Him.

Because He's right there with you—now and always.

If your life is difficult, you might want to talk it over with God in a prayer such as this one:

Dear God,

Thank you for holding me in the palm of your hand and giving me the strength to endure. I know you will accomplish your divine purpose even when I struggle to do my part. Help me to see my circumstances as an opportunity to be a blessing to others. Help me show them who you are through a loving smile and kind words. From the bottom of my heart I trust you, Lord, because I have your word that you are with me every step of the way and will never leave me nor forsake me.

In Jesus' name,

Amen

"Surely goodness and love will follow me
all the days of my life,
and I will dwell in the house of the Lord forever."
Psalm 23:6

CHAPTER 9

Trusting God When Life is Difficult

Have you ever wondered what God was up to in your life, and how in the world you were going to get through it? I know that's what Matt and Rebecca wondered when the healthy baby they prayed for was born with multiple disabilities. I know that's what my dear friend with Parkinson's disease wonders.

You might think of this chapter as a small Bible study because it is woven through with examples of God's love in people's lives. It's a chapter with Bible-based "recipes" for building your faith in God. Please let some of these things I share become part of your personal checklist of reasons why you can trust God, especially in times of crisis. It was a faith building time for me as I wrote this portion of the book, and I pray it will be the same for you as you read it!

Over the Moon

When I became a Christian at age 46, I was so thankful I belonged to God and so in awe of Jesus dying on the cross to save me from hell that I was able to trust God for everything. I was so over the moon with gratitude that I actually didn't worry about anything.

For a while. For quite a while, actually.

Now I look back and think, "How was that possible?" It's called the 'honeymoon period' of being a new Christian. For one thing, God was on my mind all the time. For another, I was reading the Bible every day, learning about Jesus and talking to Him. I was also busy trying to be a Christian example to my husband, my boys, and my friends. Trusting God was easy.

I remember the first time I was a Christian in my dreams. It was a very stormy night with a tornado watch in our area. I had always heard that a tornado sounds like an approaching train. Charlie was traveling for work, Steve was in college, and Matt was sleeping downstairs. We had determined the southwest corner of the lower level (Matt's bedroom) to be the safest place in case of a tornado. And there were times over the years when we all went to that bedroom because a tornado had been sighted nearby.

That particular night, however, I was sound asleep on the main floor when I heard the roar of a tornado that seemed to be almost on top of us. My heart was pounding when—in my dream—I said to God, "It's all right if you're going to take me to heaven, but please, Lord, protect Matt downstairs!" Then I woke up, realized I had been dreaming and smiled from ear to ear because now I was even praying to God while dreaming! I was excited that I had trusted God in a scary situation.

For years I'd had an inordinate fear of flying. It was a combination of being afraid the plane would crash, combined with nausea. Poor Charlie. I landed in the airplane bathroom the first time we flew to Europe. The stewardess knocked on the door and told me to return to my seat, but I didn't; and she left me there. Another time I was dizzy and laid on the floor; passengers had to step over me to deplane. Charlie carried 2-year-old Steve off the plane and pretended he didn't know me!

I tried hypnosis for help to overcome my fear. I remember sitting there as the guy was trying to hypnotize me thinking, "This is silly—it's never going to work." And it didn't.

Once, we were in California and had a flight back to Michigan the next morning. I woke up during the night and was a nervous wreck about flying. Charlie said, "Take a Xanax and lie down!"

After meeting Jesus, however, I was instantaneously cured! I didn't know it until the first time we had tickets to go somewhere, when suddenly I realized I wasn't afraid. The reason? I knew I was going to heaven if the plane crashed. In fact, my motto ever since has been, "If the plane goes down, I go up!"

"Do not be anxious about anything, but in everything, by prayer and petition, with thanksgiving, present your requests to God. And the peace of God, which transcends all understanding, will guard your hearts and your minds in Christ Jesus."
Philippians 4:6-7

Bulletproof Faith

Years ago, I heard a humorous Christian song on the radio: "Why Pray When You Can Worry?" I loved that song because the opposite made perfect sense. It seemed so simple—you just pray and then you don't worry! With my new "black and white" faith, I was able to put my worrywart alter ego out of commission and trust God with my life, no matter what was happening. And life was a whole lot better when I was not anxious all the time.

However, the bliss of a worry-free life didn't last. I don't know exactly how I let it happen, but the devil began poking holes in my faith with those old "what if?" questions, and slowly but surely, I slid back into the sin of worrying. My carefree days turned into worry filled nights.

The gift of amazing faith where I could trust Jesus with my life at all times was slipping away. And I wanted it back! In fact, I have been working hard ever since to keep a grip on it. I have it each time I fly but I want it on the ground! I have it when I dream, and I want it when I'm awake! If I don't have a handle on trusting God all the time, what will I do if I really have something to worry about?

I decided to make a project of shoring up my faith so I could take full advantage of the blessings and joy of living every day as a Christian. I don't want my mind to be occupied with worry and thereby miss the beauty of a life lived walking and talking with Jesus. Why should I be anxious about anything when He has all the answers?

In fact, that's the reason for this book. I want to share what I've learned and why Jesus is perfectly trustworthy—why we can leap into His arms with reckless abandon, trusting Him with the details, the reasons, and the results for everything that happens.

I found an incredible Bible verse that I've read before but suddenly saw in a new light. In this verse, God tells us what He thinks about faith and what our faith is worth. It's worth more than gold!

"In this you greatly rejoice, though now for a little while you may have had to suffer grief in all kinds of trials. These have come so that your faith—of greater worth than gold, which perishes even though refined by fire— may be proved genuine and may result in praise, glory and honor when Jesus Christ is revealed."
1 Peter 1:6-7

From this verse I saw that my faith may be tested in all kinds of trials, but it can also prove to be indestructible, and therefore, worth more than gold. That's what I want. Faith that won't bend, crumble, or fold. The question is: How do you and I get it?

After 30 years of studying the Bible, these are the five building blocks I'm using now to reinforce my faith in the trials of my life:

1) I will begin with the fact that since Jesus was willing to die for me there's just no telling what else He can and will do for me. I'm His, and that calms me down.

2) There's His unshakable love and compassion that is very reassuring. Mountains may be shaken, but not His love for me.

3) He will be right there with me wherever I am. Whatever distress I must face, knowing I'm not alone gives me comfort.

4) My favorite building block is how strong He is when I am weak. No matter how injured or bewildered I may be, He holds more power over my circumstances than anybody else. This relieves the fear in my gut.

5) I pray and place myself in God's Hands, trusting Him against all odds. A peace that surpasses human understanding floods my heart. This gift allows me to rest.

I'm so grateful God has continued to show me His attributes and His tender heart as I search His Word for reassurance. Trials will always occur, and I know that making a list of the building blocks of faith is a right and useful exercise. Create a list like this for yourself and join me in gratitude to God for the many ways to reinforce faith.

"'With man this is impossible,
but with God all things are possible.'"
Matthew 19:26

"Now may the God of peace himself give you peace
at all times and in every way."
2 Thessalonians 3:16

Truth on the Wall

During the years that Charlie and I lived in Michigan, we had the most beautiful painting hanging on a wall in our kitchen. My best friend Kathy was the one who painted it; she paints stunning flowers! Every morning when I walked into the kitchen and saw Kathy's painting, my day was brightened and blessed. Now, in Arizona, it's hanging on a wall in my writing studio. It still makes me smile.

There was a series on HGTV that Charlie and I enjoyed watching: "Fixer Upper," with Chip and Joanna Gaines, of Waco, Texas. In her interior designs on many shows, Joanna featured the metal wall art of Jimmy Don Holmes, an artist who is also from Texas. He custom designs signs and wall art to say what his clients want to say, and the words are cut through metal by a unique plasma-cutting process.

I decided I wanted one of Jimmy Don's signs in our Arizona kitchen with inspirational truth for trusting God, for me and anyone else who might see it. I chose the Bible verses I wanted and arranged them the way I thought was best.

One day when we were in Texas, Charlie and I drove to Waco to see the Silos and the Magnolia restaurant, both businesses owned by the Gaines. We also visited JDH Iron Designs. I showed Jimmy Don what I wanted, and he said my project would have to be at least eight feet tall and four feet or more in width! I was hoping for something half that size!

Jimmy Don looked at me and said, "Can you make your point in fewer words?" His challenge was a blessing because you'll soon see that my new version has been revised from what was to be on the eight-foot version, (which is still beautiful truth).

This is the original version, taken from the following Bible verses: Isaiah 43:1-2, Jeremiah 31:3, Romans 4:18-21, Romans 8:28, 2 Peter 3:18, Luke 18:1, Job 9:10.

"FEAR NOT, for I have redeemed you.
I have called you by name; you are mine.
When you go through deep waters
I will be with you.
I have loved you with an everlasting love."

"BELIEVE, against all hope, and do not waver.
Give glory to God, being fully persuaded that
God has power to do what He has promised."

"KNOW, in all things God works for the good
Of those who love Him and have been called
According to His purpose."

"GROW, in the grace and knowledge
Of our Lord and Savior, Jesus Christ.

"PRAY, always, and do not give up.
He performs wonders that cannot be fathomed
Miracles that cannot be counted."

My new version has been forming in my mind throughout
the writing of this book, and here is the draft of it:

"JESUS
He's right here, and He loves me.
He won't leave—He's in charge!
He has called me to "this"
and He has a purpose.
He counts me faithful
to trust Him and not worry.
His timing is perfect.
And His way is always best."

Behind the Scenes

There is another huge building block that you and I can use
to have unflinching faith, and that is this: The Bible says
God is always working behind the scenes to weave things
together for good for those who love Him (Romans 8:28). It's
fascinating to think He is invisible, but He's right there with
you and me all the time, just as he was with Joseph in the
first book of the Bible. Then and now—no difference—He's
working in your life like He was in Joseph's.

God worked out His purposes during Joseph's life, and you
can watch Him do it. You'll see Him steering events toward
a remarkably widespread blessing, even a blessing you and
I can apply to our lives today

Joseph was his father's favorite, and his older brothers
hated him. Joseph was given a special coat, one that was
hand-made by his father. To add fuel to the fire of jealousy
that surrounded him, Joseph had dreams that he shared
with his brothers, telling them that someday he would be in
a position of rulership over them.

The brothers' hatred for Joseph spiraled out of control.
They began to plot how they could get rid of him and

explain his absence to their father. To themselves they said, "Then we'll see what becomes of his dreams!"

A long way from home one day, the brothers took Joseph's coat from him and threw him into a deep pit. Later, they sold their brother to a band of merchants who were traveling to Egypt. They dipped the prized coat in an animal's blood and lied to their father about what happened to Joseph.

In Egypt, Joseph was purchased by Potiphar, a high-ranking officer of the Pharaoh. The Bible says the Lord was with Joseph, and he prospered in the house of his Egyptian master. In fact, when Potiphar noticed that the Lord gave Joseph success in everything he did, he put Joseph in charge of his entire household and property. The blessing of the Lord was then extended to everything Potiphar had (Genesis 39:2-5).

Joseph was personable and handsome. Potiphar's wife one day asked Joseph to sleep with her. The musical, "Joseph and the Amazing Technicolor Dream Coat" told the story all wrong when they portrayed Potiphar throwing Joseph in prison for sleeping with his wife. The Bible says Joseph didn't sleep with Potiphar's wife. Joseph told her that her husband had been so good to him he couldn't do such a wicked thing as to sleep with her, which would also be a sin against God. Out of spite, she accused him of pursuing her, and he was thrown in prison for something he didn't do.

The Lord was with Joseph, even in prison, and caused the warden to notice his leadership qualities. The warden put Joseph in charge of the other prisoners and all administrative duties. After a few years, when it seemed Joseph had been forgotten in prison, Pharaoh, the king of Egypt, had a dream that none of the wise men or magicians in Egypt could interpret. Pharaoh's cupbearer, who had spent time in prison with Joseph, told Pharaoh about

Joseph's ability to interpret dreams and Pharaoh immediately sent for him.

Pharaoh said he'd heard that Joseph could understand dreams.

Joseph said, "I cannot. But God will give you an answer."

After Joseph heard Pharaoh's dreams, he told him, "God is telling you in advance what He is going to do. There will be seven years of great prosperity in Egypt followed by seven years of great famine." He said the land would be destroyed by famine, and suggested Pharaoh put a wise man in charge of collecting and storing crops during the good years in order to have food for the years of famine.

Because Pharaoh saw that God had shown this to Joseph, and there wasn't anyone else as wise as Joseph, he put him in charge. In fact, Joseph was second in command, and answered only to Pharaoh. Pharaoh gave him a wife; two sons were born to Joseph and his wife. Joseph praised God saying, "God has made me fruitful in this land of my grief" (Genesis 41:52).

Remember the brothers and Joseph's father? They were also going through a famine in Israel. Jacob, Joseph's father, heard there was grain for purchase in Egypt. He sent his ten oldest sons to buy grain for the family. Since Joseph was in charge of selling the grain, they came and bowed before him. He recognized them, but they didn't recognize him!

Joseph asked them questions and they told him there were twelve brothers. "The youngest is now with our father, and one is no more" (Genesis 42:13). Joseph accused them of being spies, which they denied. To prove themselves honest, Joseph told them to leave one of the brothers, Simeon, in Egypt, while the others went back to get their youngest brother, Benjamin.

To themselves, they said, "This is happening to us because of what we did to Joseph. We saw his anguish and heard him beg for his life, but we didn't listen." Then they agreed to go back for Benjamin, and Joseph sent his nine brothers home with food for their families.

Having no idea God was behind this request and was working everything out in his favor, the father, Jacob, at first refused to send Benjamin back with his sons. He said, "Everything is against me! Joseph is gone, Simeon is gone, and now you want to take Benjamin!" But when there was no food left, Jacob agreed.

The story of Joseph seeing Benjamin for the first time in so many years is rich with emotion and tears. Finally, when Joseph couldn't stand it any longer, he told his brothers who he was. In Genesis 45:3 he said, "I am Joseph! Is my father still living?"

The brothers were so terrified they couldn't answer!

But Joseph continued, "I am your brother, the one you sold into Egypt. Do not be distressed because it was to save lives that God sent me ahead of you" (Genesis 45:5).

Pharaoh then instructed Joseph to move his father, brothers, and their families to Egypt. Joseph gave them carts, provisions, food, silver, clothing, and donkeys for the journey. When Jacob was told that Joseph was alive and the ruler of all Egypt, he didn't believe it.

After he heard the whole story, Jacob said, "I am convinced. I will go and see him before I die." He did, and then lived in Egypt until he died.

After Jacob's death, the brothers were afraid for their lives, thinking now that their father was gone, maybe Joseph held a grudge and would pay them back for what they'd done to him. They threw themselves down before Joseph and offered to be his slaves.

Now this is the best part of the whole story which, by the way, is a true story because the Bible is true, and because Joseph's father, Jacob, and brother, Judah, are in the bloodline of Jesus Christ. What Joseph said to his brothers is the most beautiful statement of forgiveness and of God's work behind the scenes that anyone could ever hope to hear. This is a treasure for you today, because it illustrates how God is always working in your life.

> *"Joseph said to them, 'Am I in the place of God?*
> *You intended to harm me, but God intended it for good*
> *to accomplish what is now being done,*
> *the saving of many lives.*
> *So, then, don't be afraid,*
> *I will provide for you and your children.'*
> *And he reassured them and spoke kindly to them."*
> Genesis 50:19-21

God may be unseen, but He was in complete control of Joseph's life. On page 266 of Walking with God through Pain and Suffering, pastor Timothy Keller wrote: "Very seldom do we glimpse even a millionth of the ways that God is working all things together for good for those who love God. But he is, and therefore you can be assured he will not abandon you."[5]

Looking for Insight

In a Bible study, you might be asked to look for things in Joseph's story that remind you of life in general today. You could begin by saying that his original family was dysfunctional. The Bible says Joseph's brothers hated him when they saw that their father loved him more than any of them. Playing favorites hurts others. And, if Joseph himself had any idea about how his brothers felt, he probably should have kept his dreams to himself about being in a position of leadership over them someday.

For those reasons the brothers were angry enough to throw Joseph into a pit, sell him into slavery, and then break their father's heart as they lied about what happened.

Can you imagine how Joseph must have felt on the merchant caravan, wondering what would happen to him in Egypt? Angry or not, however, Joseph chose to live honorably—so much so that the man who bought him (Potiphar) could see that God was the one who gave Joseph success in everything he did.

Even though Joseph was a godly man in Egypt, his life was not easy. Potiphar believed his wife's story that Joseph tried to sleep with her, and he put Joseph, an innocent man, in prison. Behind the scenes, God was still with Joseph, showed him kindness, and granted him favor in the eyes of the prison warden.

Joseph must have wondered why God allowed him to be ripped from his family, sold as a slave, and now imprisoned for years. Don't you sometimes wonder how anything good could possibly come from some of the things that happen to you? Eventually, after the Pharaoh sent for him and the things Joseph had dreamed about came true, he could clearly see that God had a divine plan to redeem all of the terrible things he experienced. It was to save a multitude of lives that God sent him to Egypt (Psalm 105:17). God worked everything out for good—beyond anything Joseph could have imagined—though several times it must have seemed to him that all was lost. This story is a huge blessing for us, because Joseph's faith was thoroughly tested and did not crumble. He proved that God is trustworthy!

There are other blessings here for you and for me. When you know what God is capable of doing (miracles) there is always hope! You want to know, but you don't need to know, why things are the way they are. You only need to believe that God loves you and is working everything out in the end for your good and His glory. The assurance of this marvelous fact comes when you put yourself in Jesus' hands and strive to live honorably and trust Him regardless of circumstances. Faith will follow as you rehearse God's promises and watch for His goodness in the midst of your chaos.

I have to work for invincible faith because my default position is to worry first! But it's a sweet place of respite when I find it again by remembering that nothing can thwart God's divine plan for mankind (you and me), which has been in place since He created the world and everything in it. (Psalm 24:1-2, Isaiah 44:6-8, 24-28, Jeremiah 27:5, 29:11-12, 32:17, Acts 17:24-28).

Here is some "truth on the wall" from Joseph's life:

Believe God and live honorably.

When it seems all is lost, remember:

God still has a plan for good.

When you don't know why, God does know.

He will prove Himself worthy of trust!

Always count on God.

God Meant it for Good

The Bible says that God does not make mistakes (Deuteronomy 32:4; Zephaniah 3:5). In fact, He engineers absolutely amazing results and blessings from what we see as devastating circumstances. For example, do you know about Frances Jane Crosby van Alstyne?

This woman, better known as Fanny Crosby, was born in 1820. She was blind from the age of six weeks due to the carelessness of a doctor without credentials. She wrote in her autobiography: "Although it may have been a blunder on the physician's part, it was no mistake of God's." Do you find it hard to believe she would write such a thing? Let me tell you about God's design for her life.

At the age of 9, Fanny began studying the Bible and poetry with a mentor who believed the Bible to be true and sacred, as did Fanny's family. God blessed Fanny with a phenomenal memory. At the age of 10, she memorized and could recite the first four books of the Old Testament, and the first four of the New Testament.

From a treasury of memorized scripture and poetry she composed almost 9,000 hymns and many poems. She said she composed the hymns and left them on the "writing desk" of her mind for a few days. Later, she'd retrieve, edit, and dictate them. She also cataloged all of them within the compartments of her mind. She said that, given a little time, she could bring to the forefront any one of the thousands of hymns and poems she wrote over the 60 years of her career.

Fanny taught at the New York School for the Blind. She married Alexander Van Alstyne, a blind musician. On February 11, 1915, God led her to write her last hymn. Fanny died the following day. She was so well known, people stood in line for blocks to attend her funeral.

What an incredible mind and memory God gave to her. One of her best-known hymns is "To God Be the Glory." She said she never began a hymn without asking God to be her inspiration; and she praised Him in every hymn she wrote.[6]

"He is the Rock, his works are perfect,
and all his ways are just.
A faithful God who does no wrong,
upright and just is he."
Deuteronomy 32:4

"The Lord is my strength and my shield;
my heart trusts in him, and I am helped.
My heart leaps for joy
and I will give thanks to him in song."
Psalm 28:7

There's No Better Place to Be

Communication with God can happen in many ways. You can pray out loud or silently, you can write a letter to God, or a devotional. A devotional is a writing that helps you reflect on God and grow closer to him as you study His Word and pray. Prayer is a conversation between you and God. Here's an example of how prayer happens for me:

Me: "Father, Father, help me please! I'm scared and discouraged. I need to know how to get through another day and somehow not detract from your glory but add to it. I need some Bible verses that will give me the strength to endure and trust you without wavering!"

Jesus: "Child, child, do not be afraid. You are mine! I have summoned you by name and I have drawn you with loving kindness. I know the plans I have for you. Let My grace be sufficient for you right now because my power is made perfect in weakness. Cast all your anxiety on me; I will take care of you! I will direct your footsteps according to my word. I will lead you beside streams of water on a level path where you will not stumble. Accept My blessings of peace and rest. I will go before you and be with you and I will never leave you!" (Note: The verses from the Bible for this response are: Isaiah 43:1; Jeremiah 31:3, 29:11; 2 Corinthians 12:9; 1 Peter 5:7; Psalm 119:133; Jeremiah 31:9; Matthew 11:28; 2 Thessalonians 3:16; and, Deuteronomy 31:8.)

Me: "Father, Father, thank you from the bottom of my heart. I'm putting my life in your hands right now because there's no better place I could be than securely in your grip! I will cling to you because I know you will uphold me. Thank you for your gracious answer when I cried for help. I love you, Lord."

"'The Lord himself goes before you
and will be with you;
he will never leave you nor forsake you.
Do not be afraid; do not be discouraged.'"
Deuteronomy 31:8

A Storm Approaching

Another day when I was worried, I sat with God while I was reading the Bible and talking with Him. From the verses I read, and the conversation I was having with Him, I wrote this devotional:

Today is a rainy day, with thunder in the distance. It's appropriately gloomy and a match to the news of a pandemic. Businesses are closing, airlines are restricting flights, schools are moving into homes via computers, events that draw crowds are being canceled, and people are stockpiling food. Fear hangs in the air with the low clouds.

What's the first thing that comes to your mind in a situation like this? Before I knew Jesus, I would have been terribly frightened, maybe even panicky, about the possibility of dying, losing all of our money, not having the supplies we need or access to conveniences we take for granted.

Maybe you're afraid. What are you doing when you're worried and you can only see disaster ahead? You are leaving God out of the picture, and making yourself a captive of fear. Instead, bring God to the table and remind yourself that He has unlimited power over circumstances!

He can change the future in ways that never crossed your mind. With God nothing is impossible.

Never forget God, because He definitely has not forgotten you!

My worries about the pandemic were swept away when I recalled the fact that with God there are dramatic possibilities for remarkable solutions. And even if things get worse, God is still in control. Nothing is meaningless, and He always has a purpose. I'm thrilled about the remarkable peace that I have received by putting God first. He has assured me that His wisdom and His power are beyond humanity's grasp.

I pray for people who don't know Jesus and are searching for safety in things that cannot provide any. I want them to feel the absolute security that is a reality with Jesus. At my age I have been through many ups and downs, disappointments, sad times, worries, and fears. I can look back and remember how God carried me through and eventually solved all of the problems. I may have to go through things I wouldn't choose to experience. I may never understand God's reasons, but the silver lining is that I belong to the Creator of the Universe forever. Being eternally safe with Jesus is the solid ground my faith is built upon. If you don't have that kind of faith yet, I pray you will find it in Jesus, the Savior! He will be your fortress.

"God is our refuge and strength,
an ever-present help in trouble.
Therefore, we will not fear, though the earth give way
and the mountains fall into the sea,
though its waters roar and foam
and the mountains quake with their surging.
The Lord Almighty is with us;
the Lord of Jacob is our fortress."
Psalm 46:1-3,14

Because

During the years I was attending Community Bible Study, the small group leaders always gathered the day before the actual Bible study. At the leaders' meeting we prayed and prepared by going through the lesson for the next day. Many times, the leaders were asked to write a devotional and read it as we began our meeting. I always enjoyed doing that and occasionally would write one just for myself and keep it in my Divine Medicine folder for future reference.

I did that one day while reading all of the Bible verses in the Psalms that I had underlined as favorites. Here is the devotional I wrote as I thought about how awesome God is:

Because the Bible is true and flawless,

because God is alive and so are His words,

because He spoke and the Earth came to be,

because He formed my heart and numbered my days,

because when His path led through the sea, He carried me,

because He hushed the waves and stilled the storm to a whisper,

because He is close to the brokenhearted and saves those who are crushed in spirit,

because He is a stronghold in times of trouble,

because those who fear Him lack nothing,

because His love surrounds the one who trusts in Him,

because His unfailing love is priceless...

I will be still before Him and wait patiently.

I will keep His laws in my heart so my feet do not slip.

He will be my guide even to the end.

I will praise Him and love Him and trust Him forever.

First paragraph: Psalms 33:4 & 18:30, Psalms 18:46 & Hebrews 4:12, Psalms 33:9, Psalms 33:15 & 139:16, Psalms 77:19 & Isaiah 46:4, Psalms 107:29, Psalms 34:18 & 147:3, Psalms 9:9, Psalms 34:9, Psalms 32:10, Psalms 36:7. Second paragraph: Psalms 37:7, 37:31, 48:14

I closed my devotional with this prayer, based on my reading of Psalms 86:10, 63:8, 27:11, 17:8:

Dear God,

I love your truth from the Psalms! You alone are God! Thank you for your compassion and your faithfulness. I will cling to you as your right hand is holding me up. Please teach me your way and lead me in a straight path. Surround me with your favor as with a shield. Keep me as the apple of your eye, I humbly ask, and hide me in the shadow of your wings.

In Jesus' Name,

Amen

"On my bed I remember you;
I think of you through the watches of the night.
Because you are my help,
I sing in the shadow of your wings.
I cling to you;
Your right hand upholds me"
Psalm 63:6-8

A Boy's Faith

Joel Jacobson, M.D., and his wife Virginia are friends whom Charlie and I met at Scottsdale Bible Church. They started a ministry years ago in Cebu, Philippines. It's called Child's Wish Ministry, and it provides education for children who would otherwise not be able to go to school. The Jacobsons believe an education can develop the children's God-given abilities, open doors for them, and break the cycle of poverty. The children also have an opportunity to hear the gospel and develop a relationship with Jesus Christ.

Joel, who met Virginia in the Philippines, is Jewish, a believer in Jesus, and is a medical doctor. Together, he and Virginia lovingly provide these children with Biblical teaching, medical help, and practical guidance for living life God's way.

From a video tour of the area where many of these children and their families live, Charlie and I saw housing made from scrap materials, typically one room with no doors or windows, minimal furniture. Inside, entire families were huddled together. One home had a cushioned bench seat taken from a car. These people were smiling—happy to have had a child chosen to receive an education through Child's Wish Ministry and its donors.

In a recent newsletter, Joel and Virginia shared the story of a boy who was able to trust God against terrifying separation and fear. His story shows God's protection, care, and answers to prayer.

This boy, Amadeo, had two years of high school to finish. His dream was to have a college education, which is also provided by the ministry. Amadeo wrote this testimony of his faith:

"The landowner had our small house bulldozed. He is selling the lot we were renting for many years. A broken-down portion, maybe six feet by eight feet was left for our family to stay until we find another place. My mother and my two very young half-sisters hurriedly left for our [former] small town in another province. I was left to finish the school year."

"My father—I have no father. The man my mother told me was my father told me I'm not his son. So I am left alone, with no kitchen, no bathroom, no food and no door. I hang a piece of cloth on the doorway for privacy. At night I am frightened. Our area is not safe, so many drug addicts, pushers and bad people lurking around."

"My fear came true when two policemen came telling me that they arrested two young men in my place while I was at school. Since I have no door they come and go in my place smoking and pushing drugs. Trembling, I told the officers I have nothing to do with drugs; I'm a serious student and have plans for my future. That night I couldn't sleep. I feared for my life and prayed for God to protect me."

"As much as I didn't want to bother Child's Wish Ministry (as they have done so much for me), I needed help, so I went to our center and told Brother Joel and Sister Virgie about my predicament. Right away, they looked for a place for me."

"It's been three months now since I left my broken-down house. I am safe and comfortable in my 'spacer.' A spacer is a small rental bedroom with a bed, a chair and a desk and an electric fan. I share a bathroom with four other renters. I am happy here. It's in a safe area near my school and the other renters are all students like me. I have not heard from my mother but I'm sure they're OK as they are in our hometown."

"God is good. He is my comfort and refuge, my shield and 'a very present help in trouble.' In all these challenging times I held on to my favorite verse, Psalm 3:3-4. Here in my spacer I can focus on my study and with God's help and guidance, I'm praying I will be a respiratory therapist someday."7"

Amadeo's faith is a treasure. And he has this faith even though he doesn't know for sure if his mother and sisters are OK—and they don't know if he is safe. He is able to trust God by hanging on to one verse. God does not disappoint him!

> *"But you are a shield around me, O Lord;*
> *you bestow glory on me and lift up my head.*
> *To the Lord I cry aloud,*
> *and he answers me from his holy hill."*
> Psalm 3:3-4

In the Palm of His Hand

This is a prayer exactly as I wrote it more than 20 years ago. It was lost in one of those stacks of paper I'm famous for, and by the discoloration of its paper, I knew it was written earlier in my Christian life. I don't know now what the circumstances were that I didn't like and found difficult. Oh, how I wish I did know, because whatever that situation involved, it was solved beautifully, which proves that God meant it to happen for good! Now years later, this is the perfect prayer to bolster my faith. It reminds me that He has already done so many things for me.

Dear God,

I may not like certain circumstances in my life, but when I remember that your providence covers all the inhabitants of the Earth, even me and my loved ones, I must ask your forgiveness for questioning you and not trusting you.

Why does it pain me that you are allowing these things to happen? That should be my comfort and security—the fact that you have a divine and eternal purpose that you will accomplish. Even if I don't do my part, you will call someone else to carry out your desires.

Oh Lord, you have all wisdom and all power. If you can change the times and the seasons, if you can establish and remove kings (and you do!), you can bring about your loving plans for me and my family.

I pray that I will see this particular situation as my opportunity to bring Glory to your name, and blessings to my family. Thank you for keeping me in the palm of your hand, and for making your truth known to me. If you have determined these to be the best circumstances for me and for your glory (and you can choose from every possibility) why would I argue?

Forgive me, Lord; I love you, and I trust you.

Your child,

Betty

When I read this prayer now, I see two very tender hearts—mine and God's. I'm pretty sure I had tears in my eyes when I wrote it and I think He had tears in His eyes, too. Jesus cried when His friend, Lazarus died (John 11:35). And I think it's OK to cry because my faith is still strong and I can truly say, even and especially through tears, "Help me, Lord! Who do I have besides you? I have no one who can do what only you can do."

Faith Against All Odds

One of my favorite passages in the Bible describes Abraham's faith. God had promised Abraham that he would be the father of many nations. The apparent impossibility didn't stop Abraham from believing. He figured if God said it, it would happen. And it did.

"Against all hope, Abraham in hope believed

and so became the father of many nations,

just as it had been said to him,

'So shall your offspring be.'

Without weakening in his faith, he faced the fact

that his body was as good as dead

—since he was about a hundred years old—

and Sarah's womb was also dead.

Yet he did not waver through unbelief

regarding the promise of God,

but was strengthened in his faith

and gave glory to God, being fully persuaded

that God had power to do what he had promised."

Romans 4:18-21

I don't know about you, but whenever I read those verses, my faith is strengthened just by hearing and reading the rich descriptions of Abraham's pure faith. I take them in and write them on the tablet of my heart, and then I guard them like hidden treasure! (See Proverbs 7:2-3).

Against all hope, Abraham in hope believed...

...he did not waver through unbelief...

...but was strengthened in his faith and gave glory to God being fully persuaded that God had power

to do what he had promised.

God's promises have been thoroughly tested for us and proven to be true. There's no risk in trusting Him! God's Word is alive. He breathed it into print. Great strength and great blessing are yours when you read it and believe it!

"By faith Abraham, even though he was past age
—and Sarah herself was barren—was enabled to become a
father because he considered him faithful
who had made the promise.
And so from this one man, and he as good as dead
came descendants as numerous as the stars in the sky
and as countless as the sand on the seashore."
Hebrews 11:11-12

*"The Lord is faithful to all his promises
and loving toward all he has made."*
Psalm 145:13

*"For no matter how many promises God has made,
they are 'Yes' in Christ."*
2 Corinthians 1:20

God's Insurance Plan

My grandfather, Olaf Olson, came to America in 1892 when
he was 17 years old. From a humble beginning in Sweden,
he worked as a molder in a Chicago foundry, before moving
to a farm in Michigan. He married my grandmother, Sigrid,
and they had nine children. Olaf continued working in the
foundry, coming home on weekends to clear the farmland
for planting crops and raising chickens. Eventually he was
able to support his family with fruit, vegetables, chickens,
and eggs. In time, he and his five sons built a new house
with indoor plumbing for the family.

Grandma and Grandpa Olson were Christians. Their family
attended a small, quaint country church. My grandfather
preached the sermon if there was no pastor available. I
remember seeing Grandpa's Bible next to a chair inside the
back door of their home where he would sit every morning
to put on his work boots. I can picture him reading his
Bible before going out to work on the farm.

My mother told me the story of being in the fields with her
dad one day when a man selling insurance drove into the
driveway and walked out to where she and her dad were
working. She said Grandpa leaned on his hoe and very
kindly told the fellow he didn't need insurance because
"The Lord is my insurance." And, just as Psalm 22:4-5
promises, my Grandpa was covered.

"In you our fathers put their trust;
they trusted you and you delivered them.
They cried to you and were saved;
in you they trusted and were not disappointed."
Psalm 22:4-5

Toward the end of his life, after Grandma had passed away, Grandpa got cancer. Since he lived alone at the farm, my mother brought him to our house so she could take care of him.

It happened that my parents were friends of our small town's doctor and his wife who had a special needs daughter named Barbara. My mother offered to take care of Barbara whenever Dr. Diephuis and his wife went on vacation.

Barbara was with us for two weeks. She was at an age where she should have been walking but couldn't, due to her impairment. My mother gave everyone in our family a challenge to see if we could help Barbara learn to walk on her own so she could surprise her parents when they returned. We all took turns holding her hands, but mostly my brother did it because he was at the perfect height. We walked her around the house. Barbara thought it was great fun. And she learned to walk—with an unsteady gait—but nevertheless, she walked into her folks' arms when they returned, and they were thrilled.

Years later, when Grandpa was bedridden at our house, Dr. Diephuis, who walked to church every Sunday night, came in to check on Grandpa and bring medication before he walked home. He provided the care, the encouragement, and the medication at no charge to keep Grandpa comfortable until he died. That's how God's insurance plan worked out for my grandfather.

"The Lord is my shepherd, I shall not be in want,
he makes me lie down in green pastures,
he leads me beside quiet waters, he restores my soul.
Surely goodness and love will follow me
all the days of my life,
and I will dwell in the house of the Lord forever."
Psalm 23:1-3, 23:6

Remember God's Promises

It's an incredible blessing when you receive God's strngth just by reading His Word. It's like getting a shot in the arm that instantly bolsters your faith!

"'The Lord himself goes before you and will be with you;
he will never leave you nor forsake you...
do not be discouraged.'"
Deuteronomy 31:8

"'Though the mountains be shaken...
yet my unfailing love for you will not be shaken.'"
Isaiah 54:10

"'The Lord is my helper; I will not be afraid."
Hebrews 13:6

"'...your Father knows what you need
before you ask him'
[and]...is able to do immeasurably more
than all we ask or imagine."
Matthew 6:8, Ephesians 3:20

"He gives strength to the weary
and increases the power of the weak...
When anxiety was great within me,
your consolation brought joy to my soul."
Isaiah 40:29, Psalm 94:19

"'When you pass through the waters,
I will be with you.'"
Isaiah 43:2

CHAPTER 10

How to Be Close to God

Are you still thinking of me as a friend sharing the most important thing that ever happened to me? I prayed for you before I typed the first word on the first page. My prayer was that the Bible verses I chose to use throughout the book would come alive for you as you read them—and maybe make your heart pound as you sense the great truths.

Reading the Bible is like talking to God face to face because He wrote the Bible for you! And for me. That's the reason I am encouraging you to make God's Word a daily addition to your life. As you go through the days ahead, and trouble strikes, it's an incredible gift to have living words in your mind from a living God that let you know you are loved without conditions, that you are being watched over and cared for every moment. As you read the Bible, I encourage you to form your own checklist of living words for instant assurance that God knows, cares, and will help you.

Along with believing in Jesus and knowing God's Word, it's so helpful to remember that He is present with you all the time. He will never leave you! To be able to talk to Him anytime, day or night, or breathe a quick prayer to Him that no one else knows you prayed—what a privilege!

When I prayed, "Dear God, help! I'm going down the tubes here," I didn't even know He was listening to me! Plus, I didn't think He would or could answer. But He did. He has shown me and taught me so many things since then!

That's why I need Him to pull me like a magnet into spending time with Him every day! He is so worth it—I don't want to be just a part-time follower. When you discover His worth in your life, you'll want to be a full-time follower, too.

God's Presence is Real

When I began writing this book, my confidence and faith in God grew much stronger. It happened as I became aware of God's presence all the time—as I made Him my daily companion.

Thirty years ago, I was aware of God's presence because He took me from the pit of darkness into His glorious light in one fell swoop. That experience was so beyond anything I had ever known. Afterwards, He was all I thought about. There was such a stark difference between life with God and life without God. He was a huge, always-there presence. I wanted to please Him, and I took Him into account about everything. I gave all my problems to Him.

Eventually, however, the busy-ness of life got in the way. I was healthy and excited to take on more activities. But it's a funny thing about being busy—my mind wasn't on God all the time. It was elsewhere. I didn't always have time to do justice to my Bible study homework; I rushed through it. Too many days were jam-packed. I didn't prioritize to make sure I could spend one-on-one time with God every day. When life was smooth it wasn't so noticeable. But when something happened to rock the boat, I floundered. I wasn't prepared. I forgot to talk to God about it—and I forgot all His attributes because I hadn't rehearsed them in a while.

Human beings are like that. We'd rather do our own thing than spend time reading God's word and talking to Him. I had to ask myself, "Betty, do you think God is boring?" And then I realized I could read any of the Gospels (Matthew, Mark, Luke, or John), the book of Acts, Genesis, or Exodus, etc., for proof that God is not boring! And life isn't boring either when He is more important than anything or anybody else.

That fact was made clear to me while writing this book, because as I wrote, I was constantly talking to God. I marvel that I could say, "Lord, I need a word here..." and He brought a word to my mind to write on the page. He provided me with so many words that when I re-read a page, I thought I couldn't possibly have written it by myself. If this book blesses you, it's truly because of Him, not me.

Dear friend, I pray you will take a leap of faith and study the Bible. When you do, He will speak. I pray you will have a rewarding relationship with God. One where you know He's in the room with you—where you feel comfortable talking to Him—where He will tell you great and unsearchable things you couldn't know without reading His Word. What you have been missing He will add to your life in ways you never imagined.

"Jesus answered,
'It is written: Man does not live on bread alone,
but on every word that comes from the mouth of God.'"
Matthew 4:4

"Then he opened their minds
so they could understand the scriptures.
And beginning with Moses and all the Prophets,
he explained to them what was said
in all the Scriptures concerning himself."
Luke 24:45, Luke 24:27

God Wrote the Bible and Every Word is True

It's amazing what God's Word will do for you when you read and study it on a regular basis:

You will find out God is God and you are not.

You will see that He knows everything, and you don't.

He is Holy and you are a sinner, accountable to Him.

You will learn that His Son, Jesus, died on the cross for your sins.

He will forgive you and you can't earn His forgiveness.

He loves you more than anyone else does, and that will never change!

He calls you His child!

He tells you that you are chosen!

He has plans for you and will lead the way for success!

No matter what happens, He will go before you and carry you if necessary!

You will find out His way is better than yours...

because His way is perfect!

As for a good way to read the Bible on your own, Billy Graham suggested starting with the Gospel of John. Using a Bible translated in today's English, such as the New International Version (NIV), which I have used in this book, or the New American Standard Bible (NASB), or the New King James Version (NKJV), may also be helpful.

If you'd like to join a non-denominational Bible study, I can recommend Bible Study Fellowship (BSF) (www.bsfinternational.org) and Community Bible Study

(CBS) (www.communitybiblestudy.org). Many churches offer their facilities to these two worldwide non-denominational Bible studies for men and women. You can search to find one near you.

Joining a Bible study group and spending the kind of time it takes to really be with Jesus, listening and talking, gluing your feet on the rock of His Word—just to see what it's like and what He has for you—is the most exciting step you can take into the realm of Christian experience. The good thing about Bible study homework is that it will put the necessary pressure on you to become familiar with God's Book, and you'll be the one who benefits!

Since I started studying the Bible in the middle of the Book of Matthew, I know it won't matter where you start—just that you do start! To begin with Genesis is fascinating. God will speak to your heart and mind anywhere in the Bible, because He directed the writing of His entire Book, word-for-word. Read and be blessed!

"For wisdom will enter your heart,
and knowledge will be pleasant to your soul.
Discretion will protect you,
and understanding will guard you."
Proverbs 2:10-11

"You have made known to me the paths of life;
you will fill me with joy in your presence."
Acts 2:28, Psalm 16:11

Question 13

Have you ever experienced a situation that caused you to go over and over the details as you worried about the outcome? I think many people have experienced waking up in the middle of the night unable to turn off their racing minds so they can go back to sleep.

When I got my first iPhone years ago, it was so much fun learning about its capabilities. Immediately it began competing for my attention, and before long, it consumed my time with a very aptly named game: Spider Solitaire! I hadn't played solitaire in years, and the new format was fascinating. But, like a spider, the game swept me into its web, and soon I realized I was caught, playing the virtual card game every spare minute. And the consequences were disturbing. I was forced to play the game all night long in my head. Awake or asleep, it was there.

Now you may be thinking, "Why didn't you stop playing it?"

Well, as always, Satan targeted my weaknesses. I have a propensity for certain addictions. I hated that I had to play the game all night in my mind, but I loved it during the day and didn't want to give it up. Whenever I let anything like that get in the way of spending quality time with God and my Bible study homework, God finds a way to bring it to my attention.

And then along came question 13 in our Bible study homework. We were asked to write a letter to ourselves from Jesus about something personally pertinent in our lives at that particular time.

I put off doing it because I was too busy playing solitaire! But then, as only God can do, He arranged a time on the last possible day before class for me to pray and write the letter.

Charlie had gone to the grocery store and could have come home at any moment, the landscapers were in the yard and could have distracted me with their loud blowers, but God kept that time period completely distraction free so He could impress upon me something very important.

The letter I wrote (below) is part of this devotional because He motivated me to share it. I'm not saying playing games on your phone is a sin for you as it was for me. But maybe, from time to time, you will have something that comes between you and the Lord, like I did. Here is the letter:

My child,

Return to me as your first love. Love me with your whole heart. Refuse to be lured by idols—things that tear you away from me and rob you of valuable time and valuable sleep—things that capture your mind and literally hold it prisoner. Think of the waste. When I could be talking to you, your mind is locked up with a game you can't turn off or a problem you haven't talked to me about or trusted me to take care of, or, daydreams that are pure folly.

Do you really want that? Do you want to miss what I would be telling you but can't because your mind is unavailable? I want to be your constant companion—to tell you how to be the person I created you to be, to show you things you never imagined you'd see, to use you in exciting ways you would not think possible!

Return to me; let my Holy Spirit govern your thoughts and your actions. No more wasting precious time—I have plans for you—plans for your joy and love to spill over on to others, winning them to my Kingdom. Trust me, my child, trust me!

"And whatever happens, conduct yourself in a manner worthy of the Gospel of Christ.

I raised you up for this very purpose—that I might display My power in you and that My name might be proclaimed in all the earth.

"Remember, you] are the work of My hands,

for the display of My splendor'"

(Philippians 1:27, Romans 9:17, Isaiah 49:3).

Don't forget I love you.

Your Savior and your friend,

Jesus

As soon as Jesus finished telling me that and reminding me of those verses, my husband came home, and life went on—with one major change. You can probably guess what it was—no more Spider Solitaire. I deleted it. The Great Physician used His Word, which is sharper than any double-edged sword, to cut it out of my life.

God gives you the ability to kick sin out the door, and sometimes He even does it for you! Without God, you only have your own willpower, which can be a losing battle when Satan is involved. But God is a surgeon. He skillfully gets you to address the issue, then gives you the strength to eradicate it, or He removes it Himself. The result is a feeling of great relief from the bondage it was.

Oh sure, the desire to play the game didn't leave right away, but I immediately saw the benefit of giving it up, and I felt the relief of its absence, with Jesus' presence in its place. Now when anything creeps in and takes my focus away from personal time with Jesus, I work to redirect my priorities, because I treasure, and I need, my one-on-one time with Him!

Thank you, Lord. I'm free and I'm all yours again!

"Those who seek the Lord, lack no good thing."
Psalm 34:10

"Dear children, keep yourselves from idols."
1 John 5:21

Day Planner

It took years of studying the Bible before it dawned on me that since God knows the plans He has for me, I should let Him tell me every day what those plans are! It occurred to me that I'm missing out on some pretty incredible things if He isn't my day planner.

I thought I was pretty much living the way God wanted me to by learning about Him and trying to be a good Christian. I still made my own plans and decisions that I presumed were OK with Him, if I even thought about that at all. Now, I see clearly that since the aim in life is God's[8] and not mine, I need to ask Him what His aim is! And I must drop everything to follow Him and carry it out. Here's an example: One day a friend called me. She was upset and crying, saying she was unhappy in her marriage and she wanted to divorce her husband. After the call, I heard God tell me I was working for Him at that moment, and to go to her house to help her see His plan for marriage. By God's grace, she listened to the words the Holy Spirit gave to me. She reconsidered, and she and her husband are still married and much happier today.

Another example is from our son Steve. He said a client at his law practice made a comment that he saw as an opportunity to talk to her about Jesus. He felt God tap him on his shoulder and tell him to go ahead—that she was on God's time clock now, not his. It was all God's endeavor, Steve said. And He was blessed to be able to answer her questions and help her say yes to Jesus.

You might think about it this way: When you are a Christian, Jesus' Holy Spirit is right there with you and will never leave you. Since He knows what's going on anyway, the prudent thing to do is talk to Him about everything. Ask Him to make His goals and timing clear to you. This takes practice. If you remember to talk to Jesus every day, your life will honor Him, especially when unexpected things come up in your life.

When your thoughts line up with His thoughts, and when your words are supplied by Him, He will take you places that will either astonish and thrill you, or calm you and reassure you. You will be blessed, and other people will be, too!

What this means to me is that I don't come first—ever—He does. I don't plan and make decisions, He does. I should always think, "I will ask Jesus about this."

And why?

Because His way is perfect. Mine isn't. "And the wisdom of this world is foolishness in His sight"

(1 Corinthians 3:19). I may not realize just how foolish it is. Many times, I ask God to make His will clear to me by creating an uncomfortable feeling deep inside if I should refrain from thinking, saying, planning or doing something. Other times I don't even have to ask—He clearly puts up a "stop" sign. Then I try not to override His decision!

There are times I have done just that—gone against the red flag from God. For example, during a conversation with others I suddenly think of something to say and I can't wait to say it! And just as suddenly, the red flag goes up. I've even said to God, "But I think I should say this." Imagine my impertinence! When I have gone ahead and said what I thought was so excellent, can you guess what happened? The conversation took a turn that I did not see coming and led into an area where I did not want to be at all! Whenever that happens, I am immediately sorry. There's always a consequence and a lesson to be learned when I ignore God's wisdom!

The bottom line is this: Talk to God! Talk with God! Listen to God's wisdom! I believe that all of life, every circumstance, is for the purpose of knowing Jesus, loving Him, and bringing Glory to His Name. My prayer is that I can do that until I am with Him in person, having the kind of faith against all odds that is worth more than gold. Oh, the unimaginable wonders of daily living out God's personal plan for you and for me!

"He calls his own sheep by name and leads them out...
he goes on ahead of them,
and his sheep follow him because they know his voice."
John 10:3-4

"I am the vine; you are the branches.
If a man remains in me and I in him,
he will bear much fruit;
apart from me you can do nothing."
John 15:5

Note to Self

One day I left the house to run some errands. As I was driving, I realized I was not grateful to God that it was a beautiful day to be out and about. I wasn't thankful either that I was healthy and able to do what needed to be done. No, I was in a negative mood, stewing about something I should have left securely in God's hands. I needed an attitude adjustment! When I got home, I decided to write a quick poem that I could memorize and recite to myself anytime that I might need a change of mind. Maybe it will cheer your heart like it does mine:

He is Alive!
And I'm His!
Oh, happy day, happy day!

He loves me.
He's with me.
He's got my back.

So why am I dreading?
Fretting?
Complaining?

Stop that!
Take every thought captive
and turn it upwards.

Ask Him what to think,
what to do,
what to say.

Do not be deceived
by opposing ideas
that are falsely called knowledge.

His Way is perfect.
His Word is flawless.
Trust Him.
And thank Him.

He's got your day planned.
You're here for a reason:
to be a blessing to others
while displaying His splendor.
Get cracking!
Do it with grace!

Pilot

A friend of ours who was an airline pilot said for years he liked the idea that God was his co-pilot on every flight. But one day he realized that's all wrong! He needed God to be his pilot—at all times!

When God is your pilot, you can take comfort knowing that He is absolutely in control when your circumstances are out of control. Why? Because He knows all about them and He makes no mistakes.

"'God...holds in His hands your life
and all your ways.'"
Daniel 5:23

"'The Lord will guide you always...'"
Isaiah 58:11

"'The Lord will fight for you; You need only to be still."
Exodus 14:14

"There is no wisdom, no insight, no plan
that can succeed against the Lord."
Proverbs 21:30

"'Not one [sparrow] will fall to the ground
apart from the will of your Father.'"
Matthew 10:29

"He is a shield for all who take refuge in Him."
Psalm 18:30

"With my God I can scale a wall."
Psalm 18:29

"'And these are but the outer fringe of His works;
how faint the whisper we hear of Him!
Who then can understand the thunder of His Power?'"
Job 26:14

CHAPTER 11

Amazing Truth

Do you sometimes wish you had grab bars to hang on to every day? On days when you're in pain, or when the bottom falls out, your first reaction to discomfort, fear, and uncertainty comes from your human side and you want immediate, tangible support.

Because you've read this far, you know how helpful knowing God's Word can be, and also how valuable spending time with Jesus on a personal basis can be. Now it's time to apply this truth at a moment's notice when trouble strikes. What will your reaction be? Will you be prepared to trust God as never before?

Please stay with me to move forward into the amazing truths and treasures you'll find while living as a Christian.

Hidden Treasure

The longer I am a Christian, and the more trials I go through, the more I have learned about how to go from panic to trusting God. My goal is to come around to God's way of thinking as quickly as possible, and to stay there with ease.

Before I knew anything about the Bible, I certainly never thought about God having answers for the problems that came up, or the possibility of anything good coming from the difficulties in life. For me they were things to worry about, rationalize, blame someone else for, agonize over, lie about, and justify. Such a mess of feelings I had, it's no wonder I was a wreck all the time.

Now I know when bad things happen, I have a choice to make. I can choose fear, confusion, sleepless nights, resentment, bitterness, anger, and unforgiveness (I hate to admit that I have chosen all of those at different times). Or I can choose God.

I don't want to sound like I'm always good at this. But I'm so much better at it now because I've learned how to reach for the truth and not let go of it; how to say no to the lies. I do have assurance from the Lord firmly planted in my mind! When bad news comes, (the kind with scary unknowns that strike seemingly insurmountable fear), I have the truth, in writing, that God knows, cares, loves me, and has a plan. You and I can nip fear in the bud with rock solid truth from God's Holy Word. It takes practice. But what a blessing it is when you suddenly realize He truly is the answer!

During a particularly painful gastritis attack when my stomach burned so much I couldn't eat or sleep, God gave me an idea. I was lying awake, wishing I had some Bible verses memorized, when God told me that since I couldn't sleep, I should get up and write down all of my favorite verses. I did. Over many sleepless nights I went through the Bible, page-by-page, and wrote out my favorites—which were already underlined. I chose 88 verses, organized them, and read them every day. They were a tremendous comfort to me while God was healing my stomach. And one night—surprise! —I discovered I had them all memorized!

For the rest of my life, I want my choice to be always one of trusting God. It crossed my mind that if I were into tattoos, I could tattoo on my arms a couple of favorite Bible verses in case of emergency. But then I thought—wait a minute—I have 88 verses memorized! I don't need a tattoo. I have the Holy Spirit living inside of me, and He will remind me of all of those verses. They are hidden treasures no one can take away from me.

My encouragement to you is to write down some of your favorite Bible verses. Start small, maybe just three of them. Then read them every morning and every night. Don't even try to memorize them; it will happen. You can always add another verse anytime. Consider His words your hidden treasure, too!

> *"If you accept my words and store up my commands*
> *within you, turning your ear to wisdom,*
> *and applying your heart to understanding,*
> *and if you call out for insight*
> *and cry aloud for understanding,*
> *and if you look for it as for silver*
> *and search for it as for hidden treasure,*
> *then you will understand the fear of the Lord,*
> *and find the knowledge of God.*
> *For the Lord gives wisdom."*
> Proverbs 2:1-6

The Bible Consoles Me

The fascinating thing about the Bible is that it never gets old. God teaches me new things all the time. A verse I've read over and over suddenly means something new to me, applicable for whatever is happening at that moment in my life. It's amazing how often it happens. But if I'm not reading the Bible and not talking to God on a daily basis, I won't see it. I've been thinking maybe the reason He wakes me up with a headache some mornings is because if He didn't, I'd be lazy and lie there intending to pray, but dozing instead and missing out on something He wanted to tell me.

In fact, some of my favorite times with God have been brought about by a headache, or a stomachache. I've struggled with both for years. Lots of times when I had a bad headache during the night I would get up, take Excedrin, and go back to bed, but because of the caffeine, I couldn't get back to sleep. I would tell God how bad my head hurt and ask Him to make it go away, and He would start telling me things about Himself that I would want to remember badly enough to get up and write them down. Eventually I started thanking Him for 'calling a meeting.' And that's when I discovered that pain need never be wasted when you know the Lord. Some of the things that came out of those nighttime meetings with God have been very helpful to me physically and emotionally.

One day, though, a headache was so severe I couldn't attend the meeting with God. I knew if I sat up, I would throw up and I needed help to endure. I took the notebook next to my pillow and tried to compose a prayer while the pain was throbbing in my head. It took the form of a poem. I love this poem because it reminds me that the exercise of writing it took my mind off my pain and put it on Jesus.

He settled me down as I poured out my heart in His presence, and let my tears flow like a river. He told me to cast all my anxiety on Him because He does care. He reminded me that He was right there with me even though I couldn't see Him, and that He would be there no matter how sick I was. He brought verses to my mind that made me smile with tears on my cheeks.

The Bible verses consoled me, and His love and compassion did not fail me.

"Your path led through the sea,
your way through the mighty waters,
though your footprints were not seen."
Psalm 77:19

"When I said, 'My foot is slipping,'
your love, O Lord, supported me.
When anxiety was great within me,
your consolation brought joy to my soul."
Psalm 94:17-19

"If your law had not been my delight,
I would have perished in my affliction.
I will never forget your precepts,
for by them you have preserved my life."
Psalm 119:92-93

This is the prayer that became a poem:

A Headache Never Wasted

My head is pounding.
I can think of nothing else.
Dear God, Help! Please take away the pain.
I don't know what to do.
Please tell me how to think.
I need relief...something to remind me that you care.

I love you, Lord,
And understand you have a reason
that's for your glory and my good.
I know you love me, too.
I'm still asking...please take away the pain.

You know pain.
Nails pounded through your hands and feet.
You did that for me.
You had a purpose then, that no one else could see.
And you have a purpose now, that I can't see.
But I trust You, Lord...I do.

Help me to believe beyond a shadow of a doubt
that your way is perfect.
You'll use my pain for good that I can't imagine.
Nevertheless...good.

Help me to make sure my pain is never wasted
as I tell others that you give me peace.
You reassure me, you hold me close,
and you wipe away my tears.
I'm hurting, Lord.
Help me keep my thoughts on you,
trusting in your love.
You're always faithful,
and I'm safe in your arms...pain and all

God Surrounds Us When We Suffer

When Charlie and I began attending Scottsdale Bible
Church, my Bible Study Fellowship teaching leader
recommended a Sunday morning class that was taught by
Fred Chay, Ph.D. called Joint Heirs. Dr. Chay was formerly
with Phoenix Seminary; now he's dean of the Doctor of
Ministry program at Grace School of Theology.

When I suggested to Charlie that we go to Dr. Chay's class,
he didn't think he wanted to. I asked him to go with me just
once to see what it was like. He did. Fortunately, Dr. Chay
was a 'regular guy' who wore khaki pants and a casual
shirt; in other words, he wasn't intimidating! We both liked
him.

For several years, Charlie and I attended church and
afterwards went directly to Dr. Chay's class. He taught
verse-by-verse from the Bible and Charlie and I received
many key truths that helped us stand firm in our faith.

In 2014, Dr. Chay published a book: Suffering Successfully.
In the introduction he describes the book as "...both
theological in nature and pastoral in its impact; for only as
we understand the mind of God through theology will we be

able to live successfully in our fallen finite world which includes suffering."

 The following excerpt from Suffering Successfully (pages 81, 83) was very meaningful to me:

"What we see is sometimes not enough to comfort us; so it is essential that we realize there is more that is not seen (than meets the eye). The story of the servant of Elisha in the midst of battle at Dothan makes the point as he saw a great army of horses and chariots surrounding the city and feared for his life. He warned Elisha, the man of God, saying, 'Master, what shall we do?'

"Elisha declared, 'Do not fear, for those with us are more than those against us.' He then prayed to the Lord and said, 'Lord, open his eyes that he may see.'

"The Lord opened his [servant's] eyes and what he saw surrounding the city and on the mountain was the host of heaven, angelic warriors with horses and chariots of fire (2 Kings 6:14-18). The Battle was won, game over.

"Often in our lives and in the midst of suffering, what we see and feel is real, but what we see is not all that is to be seen. God is the God of ends, not just means. Sometimes His means are difficult, but when we can trust His person, His proclamation, and His plans, then we find supernatural company even in the midst of His silence and our suffering.

 "And even if our Father is Silent, through faith we know that God is too kind ever to be cruel and too wise ever to make a mistake."[9]

When Turner, our special needs grandson was born, the "unknowns" were devastating. His needs were to become life-long challenges. My faith that God was in control remained firm. But I believe it would have helped tremendously if I had been able to grasp comfort from the visual of God's "supernatural company" that I now know undoubtedly surrounded Matt, Rebecca, Turner, Chloe, and both sets of grandparents. Whether angelic warriors with chariots of fire, or angels God sent to minister to us, God was there with many who were watching over us and caring for us in ways we could not see.

One night when Turner had been hospitalized, Matt, Rebecca, and I took turns sitting in Turner's hospital room so that he wouldn't be alone. We also needed to be right next to him in case the pacifier fell out of his mouth. My shift began at 2 am. I left the condo in the dead of night—a dark winter night with snow swirling in the air. Fortunately, the condo building had a taxi signal light inside the locked lobby door. I told the taxi driver that I needed to go to the emergency door at Children's Hospital because I'd been told the main doors would be locked. The taxi driver told me that was not true—that he'd taken people to the main doors at all hours of the night and they were always open. He dropped me off and left as soon as I had paid him. And the doors were locked! There was no one around, inside or outside. Because I came from Arizona, I didn't have boots on my feet and the sidewalk around the hospital was very slippery with snow and ice. Besides that, it was a long way to the emergency door, and I was afraid someone might be lurking around every corner. I asked God to protect me. I know now that He was there with "many!" And I made it safely to Turner's room.

Looking back on the trips to Chicago to help our family members thrive, there were days and nights so emotionally draining that the term "basket case" fit my broken heart. For all of us it took every ounce of stamina to give hands-on attention to a tiny baby who needed special care around the clock, while trying to make life as typical as possible for his 18-month-old sister.

I'm just so thankful that God gave me the strength to travel and be there in person for Matt and Rebecca. It was something we went through together as we hung on to the promise that "I can do all things through Christ, who gives me strength" (See Philippians 4:13).

That's why I'm always striving to boost my faith through Bible study—to be able to trust God with great confidence and help others to do the same when everything I see loudly clamors to contradict my faith. When I re-read that excerpt from Dr. Chay's book, I saw a beautiful picture of God Himself and His angelic host of heaven surrounding the servant who was frightened.

My prayer for you, if you are suffering, is that you will see how God has surrounded you with supernatural company in the midst of your pain and misery. God is there with "many." Oh yes, He is!

"The angel of the Lord encamps
around those who fear him,
and he delivers them."
Psalm 34:7

"Our help is in the name of the Lord,
the Maker of heaven and earth."
Psalm 124:8

Stick Tight Faith

Your response, and mine, when blindsided by tragic circumstances is crucial to winning the battle for the supernatural strength needed to travel a heartrending road. Will you panic or cling to God with unrestrained confidence?

The thing is, fear doesn't come from God. You conjure that up on your own by listening to voices other than God's.

Fear is a tool Satan uses to steal your faith. God says, "Do not be afraid, I will be with you, and I will never leave you nor forsake you" (Deuteronomy 31:6-8).

How then do you ward off fear, worry, and despair when everything and everyone argues against God? What do you expect as an answer when you ask, "If God is good, why did He let this happen, and what if things get even worse?" For me, I remember that Jesus proved His love for me when He died on the cross to save my life. Then I add the other comforting truths that mean so much to me: Nothing can separate me from His love. If I say, "My foot is slipping," He will hold me up. When I pass through the waters, He will carry me. He can hush the waves of the sea and still the storm to a whisper. I tell myself this very important promise: He will work all things together for good, because He has called me to this, and He does mean it for good for those who love Him. And I do. (Romans 8:38; Psalm 94:18; Isaiah 43:2; Isaiah 46:4; Psalm 107:29; Romans 8:28; and, Genesis 50:20.)

The choice I want to make, and I hope you will, too, is to stick tight to Jesus with bold confidence when things go wrong, when you're scared, disappointed, or overwhelmed. Your days of agonizing and losing sleep over a situation can be gone if you go to your Bible and read your favorite verses. Praise God with them until the words are so real to you that you are sure He is the rock you can count on, and the incredible friend you need.

Jesus is the answer. At any time. Always.

"Jesus replied, 'You do not realize now what I am doing, but later you will understand.'"
John 13:7

Add to God's Glory...Or Detract?

Facing a trial and getting through it with God in a way that benefits you and adds to God's glory means accepting that God knows what is happening, knows why, and knows the outcome. It means you have to believe He cares deeply and will bless you and sustain you all the way through.

I don't think this is easy—I just think it's the only way to survive and thrive. The reality is I so often mess up and forfeit the blessings that could have been mine. When life is good, I forget to give God the credit and thank Him for His love and everything else. When life is not good, I complain (sometimes with an ongoing pity party), displaying dissatisfaction with the One who loves me and who has said He will ultimately weave all things together for good. When this happens, I have robbed God of His glory, and robbed myself of peace of mind.

That's why the difficult times in your life are the ideal times to be grateful and praise God. Praise Him and thank Him for being right there with you, for directing exactly what will happen next, for giving you strength when you have none, for giving you peace and rest. Thank Him that you know you can trust Him when all seems lost. When you praise God and trust Him during the darkest times, you will be rewarded with totally unexpected life-long blessings that are available no other way. For one thing, a close reassuring relationship with Jesus—one you never knew was possible—will blossom and grow. Peace will increase.

So, how can you be joyful, loving, and kind, showing others the beauty of knowing Jesus in both good times and bad? By starting every day with God—by reading His Word and following it with prayer. You can set the stage for success before an audience of One—the only One who really matters. The One who loves you the most.

The goal is to add to God's glory and not detract from it, remembering that grumbling detracts while trusting adds. Dare to trust Him. Thank Him in advance for what He is going to do. Even if all you can manage is a smile instead of a frown, you will be displaying the Lord's splendor.

"Do not be anxious about anything,
but in everything, by prayer and petition,
with thanksgiving,
present your requests to God.
And the peace of God,
which transcends all understanding,
will guard your hearts and your minds in Christ Jesus."
Philippians 4:6-7

"And without faith it is impossible to please God,
because anyone who comes to him
must believe that He exists
and that he rewards those who earnestly seek him."
Hebrews 11:6

"Great is our Lord and mighty in power...
Let everything that has breath praise the Lord."
Psalm 147:5, 150:6

An Attitude of Gratitude

The wonderful thing about being grateful is that it chases away a "poor me" attitude. It's so important to appreciate all of God's blessings. Starting every day with a grateful heart will change your attitude about life in a very healthy way.

When you're trudging through life instead of skipping—when you're feeling blue—or you're in pain—make a list of the good things that you can thank God for. Force yourself to smile and thank Him. Keep your mind on your blessings, or the beauty of His creation, or if you can't think of

anything else—the fact that Jesus died for you personally—
and see how your spirits are lifted. It works for me. If your
spirits sink again, as mine have sometimes, revise your
attitude over and over. Thank God that He loves you even
when you're complaining, doubting, tired of waiting, or
you're depressed and can't understand why things happen
as they do. Then name all of the blessings He has given to
you, and thank Him, until you're trusting wholeheartedly
again!

"...consider what great things the Lord has done for you."
1 Samuel 12:24

My Prayer

This is what I told God recently that I'm thankful for:

Dear God,

Please forgive me! I'm never grateful enough for the big
things or the little things. Yet, I am very grateful for my
wonderful husband, my family's belief in you, for my
eyesight, for good food, for wisdom, for the right words
when I ask for them. Thank you that I don't have a
headache every day; and when I do have one, it goes away.

Thank you for showing me that even the desert landscape
where I live holds many hidden gems! You've designed some
very unusual and beautiful desert plants surrounding the
stacks of rocks and boulders that look as if they could fall
at any moment. This teaches me to trust you when life is
perilous. Truly, your thoughts and your artistry are way,
way above mine!

I love it that you are in charge of my life, Lord. I'm in charge
of praying and not worrying, and you are in charge of
everything else—such as what will happen today, or how to
solve a difficult situation, or when to move into the
unknown. It takes the pressure off when I ask you to make
decisions for me. And I thank you for that.

Most of all I'm grateful that Jesus died for me, an uninterested, undeserving, nose-in-the-air, lost soul! Help me, now, to be the person you created me to be—better late than never! I love you, Lord. I need you. Help me to live for you only, and to help others do the same.

In Jesus' Name, I pray,

Amen

CHAPTER 12

A Life Beyond This One

For years I've said I'd like to live in a high-rise with city-scape views and lots of bright lights at night. Charlie teases me and says, "That'll have to be with your next husband!"

I tell him I'm not having a "next" husband, but he and I may be living in a high-rise building in heaven when we get there!

Jesus did say that there are many rooms in His Father's house, and He is going to prepare a place for me. He will then come back and take me there, to be with Him. Read John 14:2-4 and ask yourself if what's there is exciting. It is when your heart is not troubled...when your heart trusts in God (John 14:1).

Get ready for the wonders of heaven!

His for Eternity

Do you remember a time when you received a very exciting gift? Something you always wanted and didn't expect? When our granddaughter Chloe was little, she unwrapped a Christmas present, jumped up and down and said, "I've wanted this my whole life!" We got such a kick out of her because her "whole life" was three years!

Something I always wanted was to know if I would be going to heaven after my life on Earth was complete. The day I found out Jesus would take me I was walking on air. What an incredible gift. I will never forget it. Finally, I saw that Jesus would have died for me if I was the only person on Earth! I believed and received my new eternal life.

The first thing I felt when Jesus came into my wounded life was security. Because of God's grace alone, and not by anything I could do to deserve it, I was given the magnificent gift of life everlasting. And I accepted the gift by putting my faith in Christ.

A "forever life" is God's gift to anyone who believes in His Son, Jesus. It begins immediately and there's no end to it! It's guaranteed by an additional gift of God's Holy Spirit who comes to live in a believer's heart and is a seal that ensures he or she will go to heaven (Ephesians 1:13-14).

"'My sheep listen to my voice;
I know them, and they follow me.
I give them eternal life and they shall never perish;
no one can snatch them out of my hand.
My Father, who has given them to me,
is greater than all;
no one can snatch them out of my Father's hand.
I and the Father are one.'"
Jesus speaking in John 10:27-30

"So, whether we live or die, we belong to the Lord."
Romans 14:8

Afraid to Die?

Before I was a Christian, I was afraid to die, but I'm not afraid anymore. Well, to clarify, I'm a bit afraid of pain if the day of my death is due to an illness, but I am not at all afraid to die because I know where I'm going: I'll be living in heaven with Jesus!

If you're afraid, Jesus himself will tell you that all you have to do is believe that He is the Savior—the only one who can save you—and you won't be afraid either. Yay!

Many years ago, I had a very dear friend who was dying of cancer. She called me shortly before she died and asked me to tell her "everything I knew about God." I was a new Christian and nervous about what I would say to her. I told her I'd visit her soon to talk in person.

Before the visit, I asked my Bible study leader for help. The teacher told me to tell my friend that the Bible says there is a life beyond this one, and to give her a verse from Romans to hang on to. She said God would open her heart and do the rest.

I brought a Bible to my friend and we read the verse:

"If you confess with your mouth, 'Jesus is Lord,'
and believe in your heart
that God raised Him from the dead, you will be saved."
Romans 10:9

We talked about Jesus and the Gospel. I was not accustomed to praying out loud, but I was brave and did it! Before I left, I remember saying to her, "Just read that verse and tell God you want to belong to Him more than anything else in the whole world."

Later, my Bible study leader assured me that God used the one verse to save my friend that day (just as He used one verse to save me).

Now, I look forward to seeing my friend in heaven!

I wrote a poem, and the prayer that follows it, for anyone who is fearful about dying and would like to be assured of eternal life:

No Longer Alone!

Feeling so very alone and afraid to die
she waited.
Someone mistakenly told her, live a good life
and if there is a God you'll go to heaven.
She worried she wouldn't measure up
and frightening darkness would be her fate.
Who will come for me? God or Satan?
Can anybody help me?

A dear friend told her there really is a God,
and the Bible says He loves you.
God knew you couldn't measure up.
We've all amassed too many sins
and have no way to pay.

God sent His only Son to take your place and mine.
He died on the cross to pay your impossible debt.
Jesus is His Name.

Believe He did this just for you, dear one.
Instantly your sins will be forgiven
and your fear of death removed.
Trust Him now...He can't lie.
He's the author of truth and the Savior of the lost.

Dear Jesus,

I never knew I had any sins; but of course, I do. I never understood you died for me; but now I know you did. Please forgive me. I want to believe in you and belong to you forever. Thank you from the bottom of my heart for saving my soul. Oh, how I need your love right now. Please help me to trust you without wavering, from this moment forward!

In your Name, I pray.

Amen

Heaven

Recently I was standing in a group of people who were talking about an acquaintance who had passed away. The man next to me chuckled and said, "Well, we all have to go sometime; I just hope God is the one who comes for me—not the other guy!"

I smiled and said, "You can make sure of that, you know." The conversation changed course right away.

So often I hear people say life on Earth in any shape or form "beats the alternative." I very much understand wanting to experience all you can from this life and not wanting to leave your loved ones, yet there's no doubt in my mind that heaven will be an incredibly wonderful place. I know it's going to be beyond anything you can imagine, and the older I get, the more excited I am to see it for myself.

Even with a ticket to heaven in hand, a lot of Christians aren't looking forward to going! They tend to think life on Earth is far more desirable than life in heaven. Bible teacher Beth Moore wrote a book called Get Out of That Pit. She wrote it for folks who are hurting, who've been thrown into one of life's pits, like Joseph was in Genesis. In the book (pages 204-206), she describes heaven in a way that puts "Christmas tree lights" on the typical mundane conception of heaven:

"Most folks agree that heaven is a better option than hell but, comparatively speaking, only a handful of Christians really anticipate their futures there. Face it. We're scared to death that it's going to be like our church services only instead of getting out at noon, it will last an eternity. For the life of us we can't picture how anything holy can possibly be lively. Let alone fun."

"Despite our expectations, heaven is where all the action is. Our present existence, replete with every sunrise, sunset, season change…is a mere shadow of an unthinkable reality. Get the idea out of your head that life in a perfected state has got to be a letdown."

"As good as life on earth can be at times, clinging to this ride is like refusing to get off the barge that takes you from the parking lot to the gates of Disneyland. I dearly love a great ending, and you need to know that we get one. The Author of our faith knows how to finish it."[10]

Oh, what a picture she painted for us. I can't wait to be there in person. When the thief on the cross next to Jesus recognized who He really was, he said,

"Jesus, remember me when you come into your kingdom."

"Jesus answered him,

'I tell you the truth. Today you will be with me in paradise.'"

Luke 23:39-43

Dear friend, throughout this book I have faithfully and accurately unwrapped for you the wonderful truth of God and His provision for the forgiveness of sins, and for eternal life through His Son, Jesus Christ. My prayer is that if you aren't sure, you will make sure by taking a leap of faith into the Savior's waiting arms. And, if you are sure of your destiny, I pray you will share your faith with others.

"Our God is a God who saves;
from the Sovereign Lord comes escape from death."
Psalm 68:20

Last Minute Faith

My sweet, talented, sister Joanne was eight years younger than me, yet we were unusually close. Over the years we shared our dreams, our joys and our tears along with a few things we couldn't have talked about with our mom. Joanne wrote me cute letters when I was in college, and for "little sister's weekend" she came and stayed in my dorm room with me. I had to swear her to secrecy about the fact that I smoked, and thankfully, she didn't spill the beans at home.

As a teenager she continued to write to me about who she had a crush on, even though I was only an hour away. When we were both married, we lived in the same town, which made getting together much easier. We often enjoyed going out for lunch. When mom and dad moved closer to us, we had lunch with them a lot.

Our dad could play almost any musical instrument, in addition to the piano and organ. Mom had all kinds of hobbies. I think Joanne inherited her talent and love for music and hobbies from our parents. She played the oboe and the English horn professionally, in addition to her career as a periodontal dental hygienist in Michigan. She had as many hobbies as my mother did. She knit all kinds of unusual things, and she made quilts and teddy bears. She told me once her favorite things to make were "things that had no purpose." But that's not true—their purpose was to make us smile every time we looked at them. For instance, she knit beautiful flowers, a piece of cherry pie, a wedding cake, and a monkey in a dress. She loved animals and talked to her dogs and cats as if they were young children. She also gave names and personalities to all of the animals she knitted. Joanne couldn't hide her gentle, tender heart.

She was 38 when I became a Christian at 46, and I couldn't wait to tell her all about it. My enthusiasm for Jesus turned out to be a big 'turn off' for her. That's when I learned how a new Christian like myself could come on too strong. When the person they're talking to is not a Christian, they can take offense because they hear that the speaker claims to have something special that the listener doesn't have—but should.

Before I came to know Jesus as my Savior, the same thing happened to me. My cousin and good friend, Ruth, became a Christian before I did. She was one of the godliest people I've ever known. She knew Jesus and spoke on His behalf as easily as she took a breath. When I was first married, she asked me one day if I was right with God.

I said yes in a rather "put out" tone of voice that ended the conversation. But, of course, I wasn't right with God and I didn't have a clue what she meant. Off and on for the next 20 years, I wondered what being "right with God" meant, but never asked. I think I figured if I knew any more about God, I'd have to give up things I didn't want to give up. Psychologists today would ask, "How did that work out for you?" And by now you now know the depths of denial that engulfed me.

My sister never asked, either. I was with her once when a friend inquired about whether I was still studying the Bible.

I said, "Yes."

Then she continued, "But you're not a fanatic or anything, are you?"

Before I could answer, Joanne emphatically said, "Yes she is!" She followed that with, "but I still like her."

Well, that exchange sure told me something—to simmer down and be very gentle when talking about anything that had to do with God. As the years went by, I tried to broach the subject with Joanne a few times. She told me once, "I'm a Christian, too, just not *your* kind of Christian!" I wanted to tell her that Jesus loved her more than she knew and wanted to be her friend and her Savior. I chickened out, thinking I might make matters worse. So, I just kept praying for her to someday be interested.

Joanne married a college professor and professional musician who played the French horn. Eventually they moved to Orlando where he chaired the music department at the University of Central Florida. She played the oboe and English horn in the Florida Lakes Symphony, the Space Coast Symphony and in the Disneyworld Candlelight Orchestra. Together she and her husband raised a son and two daughters.

And one day, unthinkably bad news came out of nowhere and blindsided them. Joanne had digestive problems, went to the doctor, and was told she needed her gall bladder removed. During the surgery, her doctors discovered she had cancer. The prognosis was not good. She had a bile duct cancer called Klatskin carcinoma.

People react to and cope with bad news in different ways. Joanne accepted the diagnosis with stoic resignation. She told me not to look it up on the internet because I wouldn't like the life expectancy (it was just a few months).

When I asked if she was going to do chemotherapy, she said, "I've got no choice." And from her point of view, she didn't; she was 65 and had three unmarried children. The chemo was rough, but she endured the first round of treatments. After a break, another round began, but due to complications, it was discontinued.

I went to visit her for a week before the second treatment period. She was still able to be up and around, and we had a good time being together. Mostly we lounged on the sofa and talked while watching HGTV. We were two peas in a pod and I'm so glad I had that special time with her. I fixed her breakfast and lunch every day; her husband Johnny made dinner at night. I will always be grateful to Johnny, because he retired from his job at the University to stay home and take care of her for the last eleven months of her life.

On one of those days when Joanne and I were both in the kitchen I said, "Don't you think you'd feel better if you knew a little more about God?"

Her dander went up right away—I could tell by the intensity of her reply, and the fact that she left the room to make sure there would be no further discussion. As she was walking away, she answered, "No, I have too many questions!"

I understood that. People often get mad at God when they're devastated and scared. I kept praying that she would want to talk about Him, but it didn't happen.

One night, Johnny asked me the question she probably wanted to ask. He asked why God lets people get cancer. Joanne sat and listened.

I said, "I don't know why, but I do know that God can help you go through the difficulties you face." Then he asked more questions and I talked about other assurances such as: God can provide strength and guidance in making decisions, and He gives comfort when you're scared, and you remember He loves you and will never leave you. God has a reason, a purpose, and a plan for everything, so even sickness is not meaningless. God is the greatest physician and healer. Since not one sparrow will fall to the ground apart from the will of our Father in heaven, no one needs to worry. He will help you and be with you every step of the way. Nothing is too hard for Him. And the peace of mind He can give to you may be the blessing you will cherish most of all.

Joanne never said one word during my discussion with Johnny, but she didn't get up and leave. I kept praying something she heard would help her.

As her health declined rapidly, she was in the hospital several times. She called me one day, upset because she was supposed to have a surgical procedure that morning and it was postponed since there wasn't an operating room available. She asked, "If you were me, what would you think about them putting me off another day?"

I beamed up a quick prayer for the right words, and said to her, "Well, I would count it as God's will. Maybe the doctor God wanted you to have isn't there today."

I expected her to shrug that off with an adverse comment, but instead she thought a minute and said, "You mean maybe I would have had the B team today, and tomorrow I'll have the A team?"

I said, "Yes, I would figure God has a reason."

She seemed OK with that.

Charlie and I made plans to go to Orlando to see Joanne and visit our son Matt and his family. When we arrived and found out the doctors had just told Joanne the end was near, I stayed with her while Charlie went on to Matt's house.

Joanne was at home in a hospital bed, and due to pain meds was sometimes lucid and sometimes not. She was thrilled when I told her I would stay for two weeks.

The next day, she asked me, "Is this day three?"

I said I didn't know what she meant.

"Well," she said, "they told me I would die in three days—or maybe it was three weeks."

I told her it was three weeks and she was greatly relieved.

Joanne couldn't get up at all and I sat by her bedside as much as possible. Our dear cousin, Laurel, came from Memphis to help, and she was a godsend. She's a nurse, so she knew what to do (I surely didn't) and she was just plain fun to be around. She lifted everybody's spirits and livened up the atmosphere in the house.

Joanne's three children came home. Everyone did their best to make that sad and heart- wrenching time as loving as possible.

Joanne wanted no tears. She wanted all of us in her room at night and would ask someone ("But, not Betty because she'll cry!") to open the cards that arrived in the mail that day and read them to her. She had many friends and cards came every day. One of her best friends, Pat, flew from Michigan to Florida and back in one day just to see Joanne for two hours.

As the days went on, Joanne slept most of the time. I asked her one day when no one else was in the room if she would like to hear some of the Bible verses I'd memorized.

She said no.

A few days later she woke up out of a deep sleep, startled and wide eyed, frightened. I was sitting right there, and the house was quiet. Of course, God planned it that way. She looked at me and said, "Did we pray the Lord's Prayer this morning?"

I said no.

She said, "Will you pray it with me now?"

Honestly, I was so shocked and thrilled, I was afraid I'd forget the words! But I needn't have worried. She led the prayer in full voice and knew every word. And from that moment on she was a different person. Her whole countenance changed. The barrier she had put up between herself and Jesus was gone, and her heart was open to Him. God had been working behind the scenes. She wanted to hear Bible verses and wanted me to pray for her. We then talked about the joy of being in heaven together forever because of Jesus. That was the good news I had been waiting for!

Another day she asked me, "How will I know when to go?"

She caught me off guard and I said, "Go where?"

She said, "To heaven?"

I told her, "Oh, honey, you don't need to worry about that. You just go to sleep and Jesus will come for you at exactly the perfect time because He numbered your days before even one of them began."

We prayed together then, and also a few days later, after Charlie and I had flown home. Johnny called and held the phone to her ear as I prayed that God would wrap His arms around her and make the transition to heaven easy and smooth for her.

God came to get her three days before her 66th birthday, which she celebrated in heaven with God, family, and friends.

Joanne meant the world to me, and I miss her terribly. My wonderful, tender hearted brother Jim does, too. We both tear up when we listen to a CD of her playing a beautiful melancholy English horn solo with the Florida Lakes Symphony, called "The Swan of Tuonela," by Sibelius.

I love knowing she is playing in God's heavenly orchestra now.

> *"All the days ordained for me*
> *were written in your book*
> *before one of them began."*
> Psalm 139:16

> *"Jesus said to her,*
> *'I am the resurrection and the life.*
> *He who believes in me will live, even though he dies,*
> *and he who lives and believes in me will never die.*
> *Do you believe this?'"*
> John 11:25-26

Silent Witness

Having said a tearful goodbye to my sister, I wrote this poem on the airplane while on my way home, in answer to her last question. I named it "Silent Witness" because she didn't have time, after she believed, to share with anyone else her sudden, peaceful joy at knowing she would soon be living in heaven.

Silent Witness

How will I know when to go
to the place of rest and relief,
absence of tears, no love of delusion,
darkness and denial destroyed?

To the place of wonders that cannot be fathomed.
Marvelous joy...a city with walls of precious gems,
each gate a single pearl, asphalt of gold,
rivers of crystal.

The place no one is anxious to see...
Perceived as boring...floating...devoid of purpose.
No reason to go except better than hell.

Do you honestly think the Author of all,
who thought up life, love, family, and fun...
who laid Earth's foundations,
set limits for the seas,
numbered the stars, and calls them by name...
do you honestly think He won't finish it strong
and make heaven erase the evil and wrong?

He says no sin there...no worry, no pain,
hurt or regret, arrogance or envy.
Nothing sinister lurking.

Imagine the surprises prepared in advance:
dancing and feasting, love—fresh and flawless,
relationships restored...never ending,
thoughts held captive...not racing in reverse.

Believe who He is, dear one.
With your name in His book,
you'll see with new eyes what no mind has conceived:
everything bad turned into good.
Yours for believing He died just for you.

Go!
When He summons you by name...
He has made you, will carry you,
rescue and love you.
Do not be timid, do not be terrified.
His Name is a strong tower.
Run to it!
Security awaits.

God Stories

When I became a believer in Jesus, I wanted to know if
my parents really belonged to Him. They lived like
Christians, but we didn't talk about the Bible at home.

Mom talked about God but didn't explain that Jesus is the Savior. Neither did our church.

So, one day I came out and asked my parents if they belonged to Jesus. The three of us were sitting in a booth at a familiar restaurant. My dad had Alzheimer's then and had just been guided back to our booth by the restaurant owner. Dad had gone to the restroom and had forgotten where mom and I were sitting. He ended up wandering around in the kitchen!

I asked my mother if Jesus was her Savior and if she knew she was going to heaven.

She said, "Yes, I gave my heart to the Lord at that little country church when I was a girl."

I was so happy to hear her answer.

Then I asked my dad the same question. It's interesting that the waitress had just brought our food and dad was totally surprised and delighted at what she brought because, as usual, he had no recollection of what he had ordered. He complimented her and thanked her as though she had chosen it! Next, his clear answer to my question floored me.

He said, "Well, Bets, I know I don't have to worry when I lay down and go to sleep at night because I believe in the Lord Jesus Christ!" And he emphasized the last three words.

I wanted to stand up and shout, "Hooray!"

Eventually, dad was confined to a wheelchair in a nursing home. Mom went to spend time with him every day. He was still good-natured, but needed help caring for himself. The aide, while helping him get dressed, would ask him if he could lift up his arm and he would always say, "Yes, I can do that." But he couldn't. She would have to literally pry his fingers from the arm of the chair to put on his shirt.

One Sunday afternoon some folks from a local church came to the dining room and held a mini church service. My mother wheeled dad in for the program and sat with him. She told me at one point the man leading the service asked those who knew Jesus as their Savior to raise their hands. She said my dad's hand shot up in the air! What a touching moment that was! I was thrilled that dad was a Christian in his dementia, just like I was a Christian in my dreams at night.

When my sister died, which was after dad and mom, I kept thinking how happy they must have been when she arrived in heaven. Oh, those reunions are going to be marvelous!

My mother-in-law also had dementia in her last years. She would ask the same question over and over, having no idea she had just asked it five minutes ago. The sweetest question she asked was, "Is today Sunday?" She wanted to go to church every day.

One day, I was sitting on the sofa with her and told her I was sad because a good friend called to tell me her mother just died. Then I said, "But, her mother knows Jesus, so she's in heaven now."

My mother-in-law looked at me, raised her arm up toward heaven and said, "That's right, Betty. When a person dies, that soul just takes off!" What a lovely visual she gave me!

Another friend of mine went to visit her elderly aunt who was ready and waiting to go and see Jesus. During their conversation, my friend asked, "Is there anything I can pray about for you, aunt Margaret?"

These were her simple but sweet words, "Yes! Pray I wake up dead in heaven!"

I love hearing these "God stories" people tell me.

"If you confess with your mouth,

'Jesus is Lord,'

and believe in your heart

that God raised him from the dead,

you will be saved.

For it is with your heart that you believe

and are justified,

and it is with your mouth that you confess

and are saved.

As the Scripture says,

'Anyone who trusts in him will never be put to shame.'"

Romans 10:9-11

CHAPTER 13

Seeing God in Every Detail

Of everything I've shared with you, I think the most exciting thing I've learned since becoming a Christian is that of looking for and finding God in everything that happens—good or bad. It's been monumental in helping me appreciate God, and also in helping me react with grace when things go wrong. Besides that, I now know that worrying is an insult to my Father in heaven!

Just as grumbling detracts from God's glory, so does worrying. Even if no one else knows you're worried sick, God knows. Would you like to join me in putting an end to worrying? Then let me show you how to see God in everything!

As I write this chapter, I'm praying God will help you and me both to understand the truth that will give meaning and purpose to the things that appear not to have any redeeming quality. I'm praying you will find hope to sustain you when you are weak and weary.

God is the Redeemer who will restore and make new that which seems lost. Because He can do all things! (Matthew 19:26; Luke 1:37; Mark 10:27; and, Jeremiah 32:17.)

Here is a summary of my beliefs that will show how God has given me relief from anxiety, and how he helps me maintain a Christian attitude and grace under fire.

With All My Heart

With all my heart I believe that God created the world and all who live in it. The Bible says He created me and gives me every breath I take. He gives me everything else, for that matter. God knows my name and my thoughts. Imagine that! He planned where I would live and prepared in advance things for me to do as soon as I said yes to Jesus—things that will display His magnificence against the muck of the world.

He also numbered my days before the first one of them began! I don't know what that number is—I can simply rest, knowing Jesus will come for me not a day too early or a day too late.

Personally, I find great comfort in knowing that God has me right where He wants me at all times, because it gives a divine purpose to everything I have to face. When I was at my wit's end, the downward spiral was designed to cause me enough agony to call out to Him for rescue.

"Surely it was for my benefit
that I suffered such anguish.
In your love
you kept me from the pit of destruction;
you have put all my sins behind your back."
Isaiah 38:17

The minute I met Jesus, and His Holy Spirit came into my heart, He became my protector, my teacher, my friend, and most importantly my Lord and Savior. He is who I live for, count on, and "report" to, whether times are good or bad.

When He allows turmoil and things I don't understand to
happen, I need to remember that if He rescued me from the
miry pit of alcoholism, He'll take care of me in any crisis.

"'I saw the Lord always before me.
Because he is at my right hand,
I will not be shaken.'
Keep me safe, O God,
For in you I take refuge.
...apart from you I have no good thing."
Acts 2:25, Psalm 16:1-2

It's easy for me to believe the truth in my heart and my
soul, but it's not always easy to make my thoughts line up
with God's plumb line. Sometimes worry refuses to leave,
and I need a booster shot of additional faith.

"'Everything is possible for him who believes.'"
Mark 9:23

"'I do believe; help me overcome my unbelief!'"
Mark 9:24

When Worry Refuses to Leave

What does God have to say about worry? I know He
says, "Don't do it." And, I think He's also saying, "Don't you
trust me?"

The one thing that helps me not to worry more than
anything else is the fact that God is in control of everything
that happens. This means He knows what is happening,
He's going to do something about it, and He's going to use it
in the end for good.

Because God's sovereignty is difficult for many people to accept, I decided to talk about all of God's attributes throughout the book to illustrate His sovereignty without actually using the word. But then several things happened that caused me to think non-stop about His sovereignty. For instance, two friends who were struggling with depression wondered where God was in their suffering. Another friend of mine asked why God would allow her to become an alcoholic. And, a young friend who was struggling with abandonment needed to know that God loves her and cares about her.

Since I went from hanging by a thread in a life that had fallen apart, to solid ground in a life put back together by Jesus, I see the sovereignty of God as a gift. It's a reassuring gift that means God knows what I'm going through, He's right there with me, He's in charge, and what He does will be for the best in a way that I cannot see right now.

Jamie Rasmussen, who is the senior pastor of Scottsdale Bible Church, wrote this summary of the Sovereignty of God, before preaching a sermon on the topic, and I've carried it in my Bible for years:

"The Bible declares, 'But our God is in the heavens; He does whatever He pleases.' (Psalm 115:3). That's the sovereignty of God! He is 'the Lord.' He is all powerful, all knowing, all good—and when you add this up it means that He is the absolute Ruler of all and that nothing is outside His control and purposes. So we ask: 'Does this mean we have no choice then? Does this mean that even bad things that happen are within His control and purposes?' NO and YES! Of course we have choice in this world—it's just that on a grand and mysterious level our choices never negate nor transcend the boundaries of God's sovereignty. It also means that even bad things are within His control and purposes. Hard to accept? You bet. But most people who understand this amazing aspect of God eventually admit that they would rather have a God who is powerful enough to give purpose and meaning amidst the most difficult times of life than a god whose hands are tied by a fallen and sinful world! With God's truth and compassion on our side, even in the most difficult times, the wonderful aspects of God's character—namely that He is LORD—will carry us through."[11]

The beauty of God's sovereignty is that it takes the solution out of my hands. If God wants me to do something, He will tell me. If Satan tries to tell me differently, there are verses to prove him wrong. God's way is always best, and worry creates needless stress!

Whether you are worrying about yourself or someone else, I want these verses to help you as much as they have helped me. As you read them, think about the fact that God is saying these words to you personally:

"Do not be terrified...
for the Lord your God...is a great and awesome God"
Deuteronomy 7:21

"This is what the Lord says,
'Was my arm too short to ransom you?
Do I lack the strength to rescue you?
By a mere rebuke I dry up the sea,
I turn rivers into a desert...'"
Isaiah 50:2

"Who can speak and have it happen
if the Lord has not decreed it?"
Lamentations 3:37

"There is no wisdom, no insight, no plan
that can succeed against the Lord"
Proverbs 21:30

"The Lord himself goes before you and will be with you;
he will never leave you nor forsake you"
Deuteronomy 31:8

"He will drive out your enemy before you..."
Deuteronomy 33:27

"I am the Lord, the God of all mankind.
Is anything too hard for me?"
Jeremiah 32:27

"As for God, His way is perfect...
my God turns my darkness into light...
It is my God who arms me with strength...
With my God I can scale a wall..."
From Psalm 18
"The Lord will fulfill his purpose for me"
Psalm 138:8

A Deeper Understanding

When I first believed in Jesus, talk of my belief
spread in our small town. I had no idea my faith in Christ
would be such a big deal to others. Later, I found out that
other Christians (along with the angels in heaven), celebrate
with joy whenever anyone comes into faith in Christ.

"In the same way, I tell you,
there is rejoicing in the presence of the angels of God
over one sinner who repents."
Luke 15:10

One day, Steve came home from school and handed me a
paper bag. He said, "Here mom, this is from 'Mr. C.'"

Roger Cornelius was Steve's tennis coach and a Christian.
Steve liked him because he always encouraged his
students. "Mr. C" had heard that I was now a Christian.

Inside the bag was a book titled *My Utmost for His Highest*. The book was a collection of daily devotional readings, written by Oswald Chambers and compiled by his wife after his death.

Oswald Chambers possessed marvelous God-given Biblical insight. He founded and taught at the Bible Training College in London. He taught in America and Japan and was a YMCA chaplain who ministered to Australian and New Zealand troops in Cairo, Egypt.

This book has been treasured by Christians since it was published in 1927, and thanks to "Mr. C" it has been an invaluable gift to me. *My Utmost for His Highest* is available as originally written, and also in an updated version. I prefer the original because Oswald Chambers' expressions are unique enough to stick with me, and his devotionals have since become pep talks that boost my faith and give me a deeper understanding of Biblical precepts.

When it looks like evil is escalating and the world is spinning out of control with no one who can stop it and no one who can make things right again, you and I need to be grounded in the truth that God is in control. God, himself, beautifully assures us:

"'I am God, and there is no other;

I am God, and there is none like me.
I make known the end from the beginning,
from ancient times, what is yet to come.
I say: my purpose will stand,
and I will do all that I please.
From the east I summon a bird of prey;
from a far off land, a man to fulfill my purpose.
What I have said, that will I bring about;
what I have planned, that will I do.'"
Isaiah 46:9-11

Living successfully and peacefully in the world when it seems progressively more difficult to navigate day-by-day requires unflinching faith that God will lead the way and walk with you and me. What a privilege it is to put every ounce of energy you and I can muster into the job of trusting God when it isn't easy! We'll never have all of our questions answered (such as, "Why is 'this' happening to me?") but if we grab on to the facts as God has laid them out in the Bible, we will find He has us in His grip and suddenly we have a purpose in our struggles—to live God's way and trust Him for the best outcome.

Oswald Chambers has greatly helped me to understand this.

Dare to Trust God

One section of my Bible has separated from the binding due to 30 years of use. My copy of *My Utmost for His Highest* has something underlined on almost every page. Truly, these are my "go to" books for life! I've shared many of my favorite Bible verses throughout my writing, and I'm also happy to share a few of my favorite quotes from *My Utmost for His Highest,* along with the date of each devotional and the Bible verse Oswald Chambers referenced:

"Notion your mind with the idea that God is there. If once the mind is notioned along that line, then when you are in difficulties it is as easy as breathing to remember—Why, my Father knows all about it! It is not an effort; it comes naturally when perplexities press. Before, you used to go to this person and that, but now the notion of the Divine control is forming so powerfully in you that you go to God about it. Jesus is laying down the rules of conduct for those who have His Spirit, and it works on this principle—God is my Father, He loves me, I shall never think of anything He will forget, why should I worry?"[12] (Page 198, July 16, Matthew 7:11)

"God does not keep a man immune from trouble; He says— 'I will be with him in trouble.' Rightly or wrongly, we are where we are, exactly in the condition we are in... Tribulation is never a noble thing; but let tribulation be what it may—exhausting, galling, fatiguing, it is not able to separate us from the love of God... Some extraordinary thing happens to a man who holds on to the love of God when the odds are all against God's character. Logic is silenced... Only one thing can account for it—the love of God in Christ Jesus. 'Out of the wreck I rise' every time."[13] (Page 140, May 19, Romans 8:35)

"The one thing that keeps us from the possibility of worrying is bringing God in as the greatest factor in all our calculations. Don't calculate with the evil in view. Don't calculate with the rainy day in view. Jesus said— 'Let not your heart be troubled.' God will not keep your heart from being troubled. It is a command— 'Let not...' Haul yourself up a hundred and one times a day in order to do it, until you get into the habit of putting God first and calculating with Him in view."[14] (Page 187, July 5, Psalm 37:5)

"What are you dreading? You are not a coward about it, you are going to face it, but there is a feeling of dread. When there is nothing and no one to help you, say— 'But the Lord is my Helper, this second, in my present outlook.' Are you learning to say things after listening to God, or are you saying things and trying to make God's word fit in? Get hold of the Father's say-so, and then say with good courage— 'I will not fear.' It does not matter what evil or wrong may be in the way, He has said— 'I will never leave thee.'"[15] (Page 157, June 5, Hebrews 13:5-6)

"When we are in fear we can do nothing less than pray to God, but our Lord has a right to expect that those who name His Name should have an understanding confidence in Him. God expects His children to be so confident in Him that in any crisis they are the reliable ones."[16] (Page 225, August 12, Matthew 8:26)

"God is the Master Engineer, He allows the difficulties to come in order to see if you can vault over them properly— "By my God have I leaped over a wall.'"[17] (Page 136, May 15, Ephesians 1:18)

"We can all see God in exceptional things, but it requires the culture of spiritual discipline to see God in every detail. Never allow that the haphazard is anything less than God's appointed order and be ready to discover the Divine designs anywhere."[18] (Page 319, November 14, Genesis 24:27)

I love the way Oswald Chambers encourages us to keep our hearts from being troubled by looking for God's divine designs everywhere, even in the "haphazard." Haphazard means things that seem to be accidental, random, or inconsistent. Don't you often feel that applies to the world we live in? Chambers assures us that God is still with us and we can be completely confident in Him. When the odds are against God's character, we can silence the logic of the world and say, "I will not fear."

Remember, God can walk on water!
"He [Jesus] saw the disciples straining at the oars
because the wind was against them.
About the fourth watch of the night
he went out to them, walking on the lake...
they thought he was a ghost...and were terrified.
Immediately he spoke to them and said,
'Take courage, it is I. Don't be afraid.'
Then he climbed into the boat with them,
and the wind died down.
They were completely amazed..."
Mark 6:48-51

"'You of little faith, why are you so afraid?'"
Matthew 8:26

"...He has given us his very great and precious promises..."
2 Peter 1:4

Faith That Won't Fold

You will have an extremely valuable asset, if you
believe what God says about Himself is true no matter what
happens. He doesn't tell you why things happen the way
they do, and He doesn't tell you what He is going to do—He
tells you who He is and says, "Trust Me."

Life has so much more for you than worry. There will be
troubles today, and troubles tomorrow, and you will need to
let God take care of the outcome. Jesus says, "Do not worry
about your life." He says that you can't add a single hour to
your life by worrying (Matthew 6:25-27). Worry is a waste of
time and won't change anything except your relationship
with God. It doesn't help you cope or trust—instead it's a
vicious distraction from living in your circumstances with
God's strength, and then being able to share that Jesus is
the reason you can do that!

Everyone else may see your confident faith as something to
be ridiculed, but God doesn't. It tells Him, and shows
others, that you know Him to be faithful, and totally in
control even when what you see seems to contradict it.

Would you like to have an exciting faith? I would—in fact, I
do, and I think it hinges on an attitude of expectancy. A
major ingredient in faith is believing that God is going to
take action when you and I pray. You can show God that
you trust Him, by telling Him you can't wait to see what He
is going to do next! Tell Him you know without a doubt He
can do miraculous things! We're always surprised when He
does something we didn't expect. But we shouldn't be! We

should be thrilled and thankful, and ready to give Him all of the credit.

My faith changed from porous to solid while writing this book. It happened as I searched for and typed lists of Bible verses about God's love and His sovereignty. Because His Word is alive the verses became living truths to me as never before. My doubt was erased. The fact that He is working all things together according to His divine plan was cemented in my mind. When I now think, "But, what about ...?" I am able to say, "Stop! Don't go there! God has a reason that is beyond my comprehension. And I trust Him completely."

My goal is to display trust like that every day, especially in a crisis. You and I can instantly count on God, whether He takes action immediately, or asks us to trust Him indefinitely. Either way, His timing is perfect!

"We live by faith, not by sight."
2 Corinthians 5:7

"Now faith is being sure of what we hope for
and certain of what we do not see."
Hebrews 11:1

If any of you lacks wisdom, he should ask God,
who gives generously to all without finding fault,
and it will be given to him.
But when he asks, he must believe and not doubt,
because he who doubts is like a wave of the sea,
blown and tossed by the wind."
James 1:5-6

CHAPTER 14

Thank You, God

You've now been on quite a journey with me in this book. Do you feel like you didn't understand everything? That's alright—you've read the result of 30 years' worth of Bible study! I didn't understand it all right away either. God tells us things slowly, only as we are able to understand. I've been praying that what I've shared will encourage you to do a study of your own and let God be your teacher. I hope you've seen that He is a personal God who is awesome, and who loves you.

A Personal Prayer

Will you pray this prayer now and make it personal between you and God? He will answer when you pray.

Dear God,

Your purposes are awesome. You give wisdom and from your mouth come knowledge and understanding. Your greatness no one can fathom. You said that you created the starry host one by one and that you call each of them by name. You also said that you created me and have summoned me by name!

Never let me think that you are not interested in every detail of my life. You have searched me, and you know me. You know when I sit and when I rise; you perceive my thoughts from afar. You discern my going out and my lying down; you are familiar with all my ways. Before a word is on my tongue you know it completely.

You have laid your Hand on me. Such knowledge is too wonderful for me! Too lofty for me to attain. When my spirit grows faint within me, it is you who knows my way. How precious to me are your thoughts, O God.

Because you love me, you care about me, and you understand me, I can trust you completely to fulfill your purposes for me. I thank you, Lord, that nothing is too difficult for you.

I thank you that my steps are directed by you. This comforts me because you want only the best for me. Help me to apply to my heart what you have taught me so that I may always trust you.

In the name of Jesus, I pray.

Amen

(For reference: Proverbs 2:6, Isaiah 40:26, Genesis 1:26, Isaiah 43:1, Psalm 139: 1-7, 17, Psalm 142:3, Jeremiah 32:17, Proverbs 16:9)

My God
Awesome is my God...
Wonderful in counsel...
Magnificent in wisdom.

By a mere rebuke He dried up the sea!
Who else can speak and have it happen
if the Lord has not decreed it?

He will drive out my enemy before me
and turn my darkness into light.
He will arm me with strength so my foot will not slip.
Though an army may besiege me I will not be afraid.
No plan can succeed against my Lord.

He's watching over me and He will not slumber.
In the shadow of His wings I will wait for my God
'til disaster has passed.
He will fulfill His purpose and meet all of my needs.
With my God I can scale a wall!
Nothing is too hard for Him!

My God is awesome...wonderful and magnificent...
is my God!

(For reference: Isaiah 50:2, Lamentations 31:37,
Deuteronomy 33:27, 2 Samuel 22:29, Habakkuk 3:19,

Psalm 121:3, Psalm 27:3, Proverbs 21:30, Psalm 57:1,
Psalm 138:3, Psalm 131:8, 2 Samuel 22:30,Jeremiah
32:17)

Safe in God's Hands

I am safe in God's hands, and I want you, dear friend, to
know you are safe in His hands, too. I believe whatever
burdens He allows will come covered with a love so tender
and so strong you will be able to feel His arms around you
as He carries you through the ravaging storms of life, to the
other side. You're special to God. He created you to
experience His love. You'll feel His love when you believe in
Jesus.

Jesus is the most important person who ever lived. And
He's still alive.

He is the most important person you could ever know. He is God. He died for your sins and rose from the dead to give you a new life that will last forever.

The Bible is the most important book ever written. God wrote it for you, and every word is there for a reason. By applying what you read to your life, God's personal plan for you will unfold.

Jesus loves you more than anyone else ever could. His love will surround you, and He will be the closest friend you ever had.

He will be your Savior!

"God, who has called you into fellowship
with his Son, Jesus Christ our Lord,
is faithful."
1 Corinthians 1:9

Epilogue

I remember the day God gave me the assignment to write this book. I was sitting in a Bible study as the leader was going over our homework with us when I was suddenly convinced that God had given me a divine calling to write a book, sharing the indispensable truth about Jesus that He had entrusted to me.

I was also convinced that I did nothing to earn this calling. God just decided to use me. He had it all planned. He gave me the idea, and He gave me the confidence to write for Him when He made it clear to me in 1Timothy 1:12 that He had appointed me to His service, and He considered me faithful. I actually cried when I read that He considered me faithful. That was a huge blessing. As I finish typing, I am deeply humbled. I can take absolutely no credit for any of it!

Remember, with me, that I was once someone who every night in the misery of having had too much to drink, said, "Oh, I wish I didn't drink," and yet the next morning gave in again to a drink in order to soothe the pain of a hangover. That will help you understand that this book is God's gift to me, as well as to you.

He was with me from start to finish while writing it. And He had you, my dear reader, in mind the whole time! I pray you will soak up the healing love of Jesus Christ for yourself and discover everything He has planned for you— here on Earth, and in the life after this one.

A Note To My Grandchildren

To Charlie, Meredith, Chloe, Turner, and Ryan, I love you all so much! You are a total joy in my life.

I want you to know why I featured Turner in this book. Because of Turner, I learned how to trust God when my heart was broken and overwhelmed by the news that this sweet baby was born with multiple disabilities and would face challenges that you were spared.

Turner's disabilities—and abilities—have changed all of our lives in some way, but especially for Chloe, Matt, and Rebecca. We adults didn't see how there could be any blessings when we first knew Turner would be different than other children. But God is a God of surprises, and right along with the challenges that seemed insurmountable, He provided blessings. That's God's expertise!

It warms my heart to see how all of you look out for Turner—even when he doesn't realize it. You, Chloe, as Turner's sister, are a wonderful example to adults as well as to your cousins and your friends of how to be kind to someone with special needs. When Turner has a meltdown, you are patient and gracious, and your cousins have learned both of those qualities from you. It's an important life skill for everyone. Many people, as well as God, have watched the ways in which you, and your dear cousins, have shown love for Turner. What beautiful examples you are!

That's why my next book will feature all of you! I would like to collect and share your stories—about your lives, your talents and activities—and how you are walking with God. Our family is blessed to have you belong to us, and this is something I want to share with other families. Imagine a world filled with families who know they are blessed by God!

Until then, always remember how much I love you. But know that your Father in Heaven loves you even more!

Acknowledgements

My first thank you is one to my husband, Charlie, who was my biggest encourager. He gave up a lot of togetherness time because I was consumed with writing for hours on end! He also permitted me to share his testimony, along with personal stories from our marriage. I love you for so many reasons, Charlie, and I thank you!

The next thank you is given in gratitude—I am so proud of our two sons, Steve and Matt. The honesty in their testimonies is a gift to readers and I am pleased to share it. They also gave their approval for everything I said about them and their lives! Thank you, Steve and Matt.

I love the way my best friend, Kathy, writes; and I'm so grateful she said yes to letting me share her touching story of finding Jesus. I thank God for the many years and special times we have had together. Thank you, Kathy, for being a blessing to so many people.

My daughter-in-law Rebecca planted the first seed for the book when she asked if she could have a copy of everything in my "divine medicine" folder. Rebecca, I'm so grateful you asked!

And my daughter-in-law Jody, when she read the very first pages I wrote, encouraged me to let my words spill out from deep in my heart. Thank you so much, Jody, for putting me on the right path!

My Editor, Mary Holden, added to what Jody said, and urged me to personalize my writing with you, the reader in mind. She drew things from me that made the book better in so many ways. Thank you, Mary, I couldn't have done it without you.

I so appreciate our friend, Dr. Fred Chay, who is dean of doctoral studies at Grace School of Theology, for offering to read this manuscript in draft to make sure what I said is what the Bible says! I am thrilled to have his stamp of approval. Thank you, Fred, for your invaluable comments.

Many others prayed for me and were my cheerleaders as I wrote: My "Thursday Girls," who are my closest friends and prayer warriors from Community Bible Study, my Mahjongg group, who always encouraged me when I needed to write instead of play, and the couples in Charlie's and my church small group, with whom we share a close bond as we study the Bible and pray together. I thank all of you!

I so appreciate my dear friend Leslie, who offered to proof read the manuscript before it was sent to be published. That was a very special gift! Thank you, Leslie.

I'm grateful to Diane Petro, who invited me to go to Bible Study Fellowship. She and I sang together in the choir at St. Ann Catholic Church, and I'm so glad she kept after me until I said yes! Thank you, Diane.

The biggest thank you goes to God for the joy of spending so much time writing with Him by my side. And also, for the beauty of the words He brought to my mind as I worked to fulfill my goal for the book, which was to say what He wanted me to say. Thank you, God.

May this book be a blessing from Him to those who read it. Thank you, readers.

End Notes

Taken from My Utmost for His Highest by Oswald Chambers, © 1935 by Dodd Mead & Co., renewed © 1963 by the Oswald Chambers Publications Assn., Ltd. Used by permission of Our Daily Bread Publishing, Grand Rapids MI 49501. All rights reserved. p. 218

Taken from Love Life For Every Married Couple by Ed Wheat, M.D., Copyright © 1980 by Ed Wheat, M.D., Used by permission of Zondervan. www.zondervan.com

Excerpt from MAKING SENSE OF GOD: AN INVITATION TO THE SKEPTICAL, by Timothy Keller, copyright © 2016 by Timothy Keller. Used by permission of Viking Books, an imprint of Penguin Publishing Group, a division of Penguin Random House LLC. All rights reserved.

Taken from a message given by Pastor Joby Martin, lead pastor at the Church of Eleven 22, Jacksonville, FL. Permission granted by Pastor Joby Martin. The Communication Team, The Church of Eleven 22, coe22.com

Excerpt from WALKING WITH GOD THROUGH PAIN AND SUFFERING by Timothy Keller, copyright © 2013 by Timothy Keller. Used by permission of Dutton, an imprint of Penguin Publishing Group, a division of Penguin Random House LLC. All rights reserved.

Taken from More Than Conquerors, Copyright © 1992, The Moody Bible Institute of Chicago, John Woodbridge, General Editor, 'To God be the Glory' by Richard Stanislaw,

permission of Our Daily Bread Publishing, Grand Rapids MI 49501. All rights reserved., p. 198

Ibid., p. 140.

Ibid., p. 187.

Ibid., p. 157.

Ibid., p. 225.

Ibid., p. 136.

Ibid., p. 319.

About the Author

Betty Simpson is one of the most addictive people you could ever meet. She was addicted to alcohol until it almost killed her. The fact that God could break through her addiction and rescue her is the single most amazing fact of her life! She likes to share how He did that, and how He also put a stop to her second addiction: obsessive worry.

After becoming a Christian, Betty served for many years as a leader at Bible Study Fellowship in Michigan, and also at Community Bible Study in Arizona.

Betty married Charlie Simpson because when he first kissed her, she saw stars! They lived for 45 years on a picturesque lake in Richland, Michigan where they raised two sons. After spending several winters in Scottsdale, Arizona, they are now residents of God's beautiful desert. They attend Scottsdale Bible Church.